In: Terrorism, Hot Spots and Conflict-Related Issues

SUITS AGAINST TERRORIST STATES BY VICTIMS OF TERRORISM

TERRORISM, HOT SPOTS AND CONFLICT-RELATED ISSUES SERIES

Suits Against Terrorist States by Victims of Terrorism
Beatrice V. Mohoney
2009 ISBN: 978-1-60692-835-6

In: Terrorism, Hot Spots and Conflict-Related Issues

SUITS AGAINST TERRORIST STATES BY VICTIMS OF TERRORISM

BEATRICE V. MOHONEY
EDITOR

Nova Science Publishers, Inc.
New York

Copyright © 2009 by Nova Science Publishers, Inc.

All rights reserved. No part of this book may be reproduced, stored in a retrieval system or transmitted in any form or by any means: electronic, electrostatic, magnetic, tape, mechanical photocopying, recording or otherwise without the written permission of the Publisher.

For permission to use material from this book please contact us:
Telephone 631-231-7269; Fax 631-231-8175
Web Site: http://www.novapublishers.com

NOTICE TO THE READER

The Publisher has taken reasonable care in the preparation of this book, but makes no expressed or implied warranty of any kind and assumes no responsibility for any errors or omissions. No liability is assumed for incidental or consequential damages in connection with or arising out of information contained in this book. The Publisher shall not be liable for any special, consequential, or exemplary damages resulting, in whole or in part, from the readers' use of, or reliance upon, this material.

Independent verification should be sought for any data, advice or recommendations contained in this book. In addition, no responsibility is assumed by the publisher for any injury and/or damage to persons or property arising from any methods, products, instructions, ideas or otherwise contained in this publication.

This publication is designed to provide accurate and authoritative information with regard to the subject matter covered herein. It is sold with the clear understanding that the Publisher is not engaged in rendering legal or any other professional services. If legal or any other expert assistance is required, the services of a competent person should be sought. FROM A DECLARATION OF PARTICIPANTS JOINTLY ADOPTED BY A COMMITTEE OF THE AMERICAN BAR ASSOCIATION AND A COMMITTEE OF PUBLISHERS.

LIBRARY OF CONGRESS CATALOGING-IN-PUBLICATION DATA
Available upon request
ISBN: 978-1-60692-835-6

Published by Nova Science Publishers, Inc. ✦ *New York*

CONTENTS

Preface		vii
Chapter 1	Suits Against Terrorist States by Victims of Terrorism *Jennifer K. Elsea*	1
Chapter 2	Lawsuits Against State Supporters of Terrorism: An Overview *Jennifer K. Elsea*	97
Index		107

PREFACE

Congress amended the 1996 Foreign Sovereign Immunities Act (FSIA) to allow U.S. victims of terrorism to sue designated State sponsors of terrorism for their terrorist acts. The courts have handed down large judgments against the terrorist State defendants, generally in default, and successive Administrations have intervened to block the judicial attachment of frozen assets to satisfy judgments. This book provides background on the doctrine of State immunity and the FSIA; details the evolution of the terrorist State exception and some of the resulting judicial decisions; describes legislative efforts to help claimants satisfy their judgments; summarizes the hostages' suit against Iran and Congress's efforts to intervene; summarizes the status of lawsuits against Iraq and Libya; and provides an overview of proposed legislation (S. 3370, H.R. 3346, S. 1944, H.R. 394, H.R. 5167, and H.R. 2764). Appendix A provides a list of cases, including those covered by TRIA § 2002 and the amount of compensation paid. Appendix B lists the assets of each terrorist State currently blocked by the United States and the total amount owed by each for terrorism judgments.

Chapter 1 - In 1996 Congress amended the Foreign Sovereign Immunities Act (FSIA) to allow U.S. victims of terrorism to sue designated State sponsors of terrorism for their terrorist acts. The courts have handed down large judgments against the terrorist State defendants, generally in default, and successive Administrations have intervened to block the judicial attachment of frozen assets to satisfy judgments. After a court ruled that Congress never created a cause of action against terrorist States themselves, but only against their officials, employees, and agents, plaintiffs have based claims on state law. The limited availability of defendant States' assets for satisfaction of judgments has made collection difficult. Congress passed a rider to the National Defense Authorization Act for FY2008 (H.R. 4986), to provide a federal cause of action against terrorist

States and to facilitate enforcement of judgments, authorizing the President to waive the provision with respect to Iraq. Congress subsequently passed S. 3390 to exempt Libya from the FSIA provisions if it agrees to compensate victims with pending lawsuits.

Chapter 2 - A 1996 amendment to the Foreign Sovereign Immunities Act (FSIA) enables American victims of international terrorist acts supported by certain States designated by the State Department as sponsors of terrorism — Cuba, Iran, North Korea, Sudan, Syria, and previously Iraq and Libya — to bring suit in U.S. courts for damages. Despite congressional efforts to make blocked (or "frozen") assets of such States available for attachment by judgment creditors in such cases, plaintiffs encountered difficulties in enforcing the awards. Congress passed, as part of the National Defense Authorization Act for FY2008 (NDAA) (H.R. 1585), an amendment to the FSIA to provide a federal cause of action against terrorist States and to facilitate enforcement of judgments. After the President vetoed the NDAA based on the possible impact the measure would have on Iraqi assets, Congress passed a new version, P.L. 110-181 (H.R. 4986), which includes authority for the President to waive the FSIA provision with respect to Iraq. Congress later passed a measure to exempt Libya if it agrees to compensate victims (S. 3370). This report, which will be updated, provides an overview of these issues and relevant legislation (H.R. 5167). For more details, see CRS Report RL3 1258, Suits Against Terrorist States by Victims of Terrorism, by Jennifer K. Elsea.

In: Suits Against Terrorist...
Editor: Beatrice V. Mohoney

ISBN 978-1-60692-835-6
© 2009 Nova Science Publishers, Inc.

Chapter 1

SUITS AGAINST TERRORIST STATES BY VICTIMS OF TERRORISM[*]

Jennifer K. Elsea

ABSTRACT

In 1996 Congress amended the Foreign Sovereign Immunities Act (FSIA) to allow U.S. victims of terrorism to sue designated State sponsors of terrorism for their terrorist acts. The courts have handed down large judgments against the terrorist State defendants, generally in default, and successive Administrations have intervened to block the judicial attachment of frozen assets to satisfy judgments. After a court ruled that Congress never created a cause of action against terrorist States themselves, but only against their officials, employees, and agents, plaintiffs have based claims on state law. The limited availability of defendant States' assets for satisfaction of judgments has made collection difficult. Congress passed a rider to the National Defense Authorization Act for FY2008 (H.R. 4986), to provide a federal cause of action against terrorist States and to facilitate enforcement of judgments, authorizing the President to waive the provision with respect to Iraq. Congress subsequently passed S. 3390 to exempt Libya from the FSIA provisions if it agrees to compensate victims with pending lawsuits.

Section 1083 of P.L. 110-181 is the latest in a series of actions Congress has taken over the last decade to assist plaintiffs in lawsuits against terrorist States. The 107th Congress enacted a measure in the Terrorism Risk Insurance Act of 2002 ("TRIA") (P.L. 107-297) to allow the attachment of

---

[*] Excerpted from CRS Report RL31258, dated August 8, 2008.

blocked assets of terrorist States to pay compensatory damages to victims. The Victims of Trafficking and Violence Protection Act of 2000 ("VTVPA") (P.L. 106-386) liquidated some frozen assets to pay claims and provided some U.S. funds to compensate those holding judgments against Iran at the time. Section 1083 seeks to make more assets available to execute terrorism judgments. It permits the attachment of assets belonging to separate agencies and instrumentalities of defendant States, permits plaintiffs to file notices of lis pendens with respect to property owned by defendant States or entities they control, and permits some plaintiffs to refile claims.

The Supreme Court has not directly addressed the FSIA terrorism exception, but in 2006 it remanded a decision based on the lower court's assumption that Iran's Ministry of Defense (MOD) is an "agency or instrumentality" of Iran rather than part of the government itself, and will decide in its upcoming term whether certain Iranian assets are available under the TRIA to judgment holders. The Court may also be asked to determine the effect of the waiver of § 1083 on pending cases against Iraq, which the Court of Appeals for the D.C. Circuit has permitted to go forward.

This report provides background on the doctrine of State immunity and the FSIA; details the evolution of the terrorist State exception and some of the resulting judicial decisions; describes legislative efforts to help claimants satisfy their judgments; summarizes the hostages' suit against Iran and Congress's efforts to intervene; summarizes the status of lawsuits against Iraq and Libya; and provides an overview of proposed legislation (S. 3370, H.R. 3346, S. 1944, H.R. 394, H.R. 5167, and H.R. 2764). Appendix A provides a list of cases, including those covered by TRIA § 2002 and the amount of compensation paid. Appendix B lists the assets of each terrorist State currently blocked by the United States and the total amount owed by each for terrorism judgments. The report will be updated as events warrant.

OVERVIEW

Prior to 1996, foreign States were immune from civil liability in U.S. courts for injuries caused by acts of terrorism carried out by their agents and proxies. In 1996, Congress amended the Foreign Sovereign Immunities Act (FSIA) [1] to allow civil suits by U.S. victims of terrorism against certain States responsible for, or complicit in, such terrorist acts as torture, extrajudicial killing, aircraft sabotage, and hostage taking. [2] The amendment enjoyed broad support in Congress, but was initially resisted by the executive branch. President Clinton signed the amendment into law after the Cuban air force shot down a civilian plane over international waters, an incident that resulted in one of the first lawsuits under the new FSIA exception. After a court found that the waiver of sovereign immunity did not itself create a private right of action, Congress passed the Flatow Amendment to create a cause of action. [3] Numerous court judgments awarding plaintiffs substantial compensatory and punitive damages were to follow, [4] until the D.C. Circuit in 2004 interpreted the provisions in a way that made further awards somewhat more difficult for plaintiffs to win. Plaintiffs thereafter largely relied on domestic state law to provide a cause of action, which resulted in some disparity in the amount and type of relief available to different victims of the same terrorist attacks.

Although the defendant State sponsors of terrorism have frequently declined to appear in court to defend against the lawsuits, the litigation has nevertheless proven contentious, often leading to the perception on the part of plaintiffs that the U.S. government is their most formidable adversary. Nevertheless, U.S. courts have awarded victims of terrorism more than $19 billion against State sponsors of terrorism and their officials, most of which remains uncollected. The scarcity of assets within U.S. jurisdiction that belong to States subject to economic sanctions has made judgments against terrorist States difficult to enforce. Efforts by plaintiffs to attach frozen assets and diplomatic or consular property, while receiving support from Congress, have met with opposition from the executive branch. The total amount of judgments against terrorist States far exceeds the assets of debtor States known to exist within the jurisdiction of U.S. courts. The use of U.S. funds to pay portions of some judgments has drawn criticism. Calls for a more effective and fair means to compensate victims of terrorism have not yielded an alternative mechanism. The issue has pitted the compensation of victims of terrorism against U.S. foreign policy goals and some business interests.

Congress passed a rider to the National Defense Authorization Act for FY2008 (H.R. 1585), to provide a cause of action against terrorist States and to facilitate enforcement of judgments, and to permit some plaintiffs to refile claims that were unsuccessful under the previous law. The provision also permits the filing of new cases related to terrorist incidents that have been the subject of previous cases, in order to permit the filing of cases in which the plaintiffs were previously ineligible to file or had missed the filing deadline, or perhaps in order to garner higher damages.

After the President vetoed the bill based on the possible impact the measure would have on Iraq, Congress passed a new version, H.R. 4986, this time authorizing the President to waive its provisions with respect to Iraq. The President signed the bill into law, P.L. 110-181, and promptly issued a waiver with respect to Iraq. The Administration now seeks a waiver for Libya and other States whose designation may be lifted. However, the Court of Appeals for the D.C. Circuit has ruled that the waiver with respect to Iraq does not affect pending cases, which are permitted to go forward under the FSIA as it was in effect prior to the FY2008 NDAA.

This report provides background on the international law doctrine of foreign State immunity and the FSIA; summarizes the 1996 amendments creating an exception to state immunity under the FSIA for suits against terrorist States; details the subsequent cases and the legislative initiatives to assist claimants in efforts to collect on their judgments; sets forth the legal and policy arguments that were made for and against those efforts; summarizes the decision in Roeder v. Islamic Republic of Iran and efforts to help the plaintiffs and override the Algiers Accords; describes the Administration's actions vesting title to Iraq's frozen assets in the United States and making them unavailable to former POWs in Acree v. Republic of Iraq and other plaintiffs who have won judgments against Iraq; discusses an effort by Iran to void a judgment against it (Ministry of Defense v. Elahi); notes the laws in certain terrorist States that allow suits against the U.S. for similar acts; and concludes that the issue of providing fair compensation to victims of terrorism is not one that will likely dissipate any time soon.

The report also contains two appendixes: Appendix A lists the cases covered by § 2002 of the Victims of Trafficking and Violence Protection Act of 2000 (P.L. 106-386), the amount of compensation that has been paid in each case, and the source of the compensation. It provides a separate list of judgments handed down later that are not covered by the compensation schemes set forth in earlier legislation, whose creditors will likely compete with each other to satisfy claims out of scarce blocked assets. Appendix B lists the amount of the assets of each terrorist State blocked by the United States as of the end of 2006, as compared to the current sum of judgments that remain to be satisfied. The report will be updated as events warrant.

BACKGROUND ON STATE IMMUNITY

Customary international law historically afforded sovereign States complete immunity from being sued in the courts of other States. In the words of Chief Justice Marshall, this immunity was rooted in the "perfect equality and absolute independence of sovereigns" and the need to maintain friendly relations. Although each nation has "full and absolute" jurisdiction within its own territory, the Chief Justice stated, that jurisdiction, by common consent, does not extend to other sovereign States:

One sovereign being in no respect amenable to another; and being bound by obligations of the highest character not to degrade the dignity of his nation, by placing himself or its sovereign rights within the jurisdiction of another, can be supposed to enter a foreign territory only under an express license, or in the confidence that the immunities belonging to this independent sovereign station, though not expressly stipulated, are reserved by implication, and will be extended to him.

This perfect equality and absolute independence of sovereigns, and this common interest impelling them to mutual intercourse, and an interchange of good offices with each other, have given rise to a class of cases in which every sovereign is understood to waive the exercise of a part of that complete exclusive territorial jurisdiction, which has been stated to be the attribute of every nation. [5]

During the last century, however, this principle of absolute sovereign immunity gradually came to be limited after a number of States began engaging directly in commercial activities. To allow States to maintain their immunity in the courts of other States even while engaged in ordinary commerce, it was said, "gave States an unfair advantage in competition with private commercial enterprise" and denied the private parties in other nations with whom they dealt their normal recourse to the courts to settle disputes. [6] As a consequence, numerous States immediately before and after World War II adopted the "restrictive principle" of state immunity, which preserves sovereign immunity for most cases but allows domestic courts to exercise jurisdiction over suits against foreign States for claims arising out of their commercial activities.

The United States adopted the restrictive principle of sovereign immunity by administrative action in 1952, [7] and the State Department began advising courts on a case-by-case basis whether a foreign sovereign should be entitled to immunity from a U.S. court's jurisdiction based on the nature of the claim. In 1978 Congress codified the principle in the Foreign Sovereign Immunities Act (FSIA), so that the decision no longer depended on a determination by the State Department. [8] The FSIA states the general principle that "a foreign state shall be immune from the jurisdiction of the courts of the United States and of the States" [9] and then sets forth several exceptions. The primary exceptions are for cases in which "the foreign state has waived its immunity either expressly or by implication," cases in which "the action is based upon a commercial activity carried on in the United States by the foreign state," and suits against a foreign State for personal injury or death or damage to property occurring in the United States as a result of the tortious act of an official or employee of that State acting within the scope of his office or employment. [10] For most types of claims covered, the FSIA also provides that the commercial property of a foreign State in the United States may be attached in satisfaction of a judgment against it regardless of whether the property was used for the activity on which the claim was based. [11] However, assets belonging to separate instrumentalities of a foreign government are not generally available to satisfy claims against the foreign government itself or against other agencies and instrumentalities in which that government has an interest.

THE ANTI-TERRORISM AND EFFECTIVE DEATH PENALTY ACT OF 1996: CIVIL SUITS AGAINST TERRORIST STATES BY VICTIMS OF TERRORISM

In 1996 Congress added another exception to the FSIA to allow the U.S. courts, federal and state, to exercise jurisdiction over foreign States and their agencies and instrumentalities in civil suits by U.S. victims of terrorism. [12] The Anti-Terrorism and Effective Death Penalty Act of 1996 (AEDPA) amended the FSIA to provide that a foreign State is not immune from the jurisdiction of U.S. courts in cases in which

> money damages are sought against a foreign state for personal injury or death that was caused by an act of torture, extrajudicial killing, aircraft sabotage, hostage taking, or the provision of material support or resources ... for such an act if such act or provision of material support is engaged in by an official, employee, or agent of such foreign state while acting within the scope of his or her office, employment, or agency.... [13]

As predicates for such suits, the AEDPA amendment required that the foreign State be designated as a State sponsor of terrorism by the State Department at the time the act occurred or later so designated as a consequence of the act in question, [14] that either the claimant or the victim of the act of terrorism be a U.S. national, [15] and that the defendant State be given a prior opportunity to arbitrate the claim if the act on which the claim is based occurred in the territory of the defendant State. The act also provided that the terrorist States and their agencies and instrumentalities would be liable for compensatory damages, and the agencies and instrumentalities for punitive damages as well. [16] The act further allowed the commercial property of a foreign State in the United States to be attached in satisfaction of a judgment against that State under this amendment regardless of whether the property was involved in the act on which the claim was based. [17] After previously opposing similar proposals, the Clinton Administration agreed to these changes in the FSIA.

After a court found that the terrorism exception to sovereign immunity did not itself create a cause of action, [18] Congress passed the Civil Liability for Acts of State- Sponsored Terrorism (known as the "Flatow Amendment") [19] to clarify that a cause of action existed against the officials, employees, and agents of States whose sovereign immunity was abrogated pursuant to the exception. The Flatow Amendment gives parties injured or killed by a terrorist act covered by the FSIA exception, or their legal representatives, a cause of action for suits against "an official, employee, or agent of a foreign state designated as a state sponsor of terrorism" who commits the terrorist act "while acting within the scope of his or her office, employment, or agency ...." if a U.S. government official would be liable for similar actions. This measure was adopted as part of the Omnibus Consolidated Appropriations Act for Fiscal 1997 without apparent debate. [20]

EARLY CASES AND EFFORTS TO SATISFY JUDGMENTS

Several suits were quickly filed against Cuba and Iran pursuant to the new provisions. Neither State recognized the jurisdiction of the U.S. courts in such suits, however; and both refused to appear in court to mount a defense. The FSIA provides that a court may enter a judgment by default in such a situation if "the claimant establishes his claim or right to relief by evidence satisfactory to the court." [21] After making the proper finding, several federal trial courts entered default judgments holding Iran and Cuba to be culpable for particular acts of terrorism and awarding the plaintiffs substantial amounts in compensatory and punitive damages. [22]

Neither Iran nor Cuba had any inclination to pay the damages that had been assessed in these cases. As a consequence, the plaintiffs and their attorneys sought to attach certain properties and other assets owned by the States in question that were located within the jurisdiction of the United States to satisfy the judgments.

In the case of Flatow v. Islamic Republic of Iran, plaintiffs sought to attach the embassy and several diplomatic properties of Iran located in Washington, DC, the proceeds that had accrued from the rental of those properties after diplomatic relations had been broken in 1979, and an award that had been rendered by the IranU.S. Claims Tribunal in favor of Iran and against the U.S. government but which had not yet been paid. [23] The Clinton Administration opposed these efforts, arguing that the diplomatic properties and the rental proceeds were essentially sovereign noncommercial property that remained immune to attachment pursuant to the FSIA. In addition, the Administration argued that it was obligated to protect Iran's diplomatic and consular properties under the Vienna Convention on Diplomatic Relations [24] and the Vienna Convention on Consular Relations [25] and that using such properties to satisfy court judgments would expose U.S. diplomatic and consular properties around the world to similar treatment by other countries. The Clinton Administration further argued that the funds set aside to pay an award to Iran by the decision of the Claims Tribunal were still U.S. property and, as such, were immune from attachment due to U.S. sovereign immunity. The court agreed and quashed the writs of attachment. [26]

Efforts were also mounted in both the Flatow case and in Alejandre v. Republic of Cuba (the Brothers to the Rescue case) to attach assets of Iran and Cuba in the United States that had been blocked by the U.S. government pursuant to sanctions regulations. [27] Iran's assets in the United States had been frozen under the authority of the International Emergency Economic Powers Act (IEEPA) [28] at the time of the hostage crisis in 1979. [29] However, under the Algiers Accords reached to resolve the crisis, most of those assets had either been returned to Iran or placed in an escrow account in England subject to the decisions of the Iran-U.S. Claims Tribunal, an arbitral body set up by the Algiers Accords to resolve remaining disputes between the two countries or their nationals. Cuba's assets in the United States had been blocked since the early 1960s under the authority of the Trading with the Enemy Act (TWEA). [30] The Clinton Administration opposed the efforts to allow access to these assets as well. It argued that such assets are useful, and historically have been used, as leverage in working out foreign policy disputes with other countries (as in the Iranian hostage situation) and that they will be useful in negotiating the possible future re-establishment of normal relations with Iran and Cuba. The Administration also contended that numerous other U.S. nationals had legitimate (and prior) claims against these countries that would be frustrated if the assets were used solely to compensate the recent victims of terrorism. [31] The Administration also argued that using frozen assets to compensate victims of State-sponsored terrorism exposes the United States to the risk of reciprocal actions against U.S. assets by other States. [32]

105th Congress: Section 117 of the Treasury and General Government Appropriations Act for Fiscal Year 1999

In an attempt to override these objections, the 105th Congress in 1998 further amended the FSIA to provide that any property of a terrorist State frozen pursuant to TWEA or IEEPA and any diplomatic property of such a State could be subject to execution or attachment in aid of execution of a judgment against that State under the terrorism State exception to the FSIA. [33] Section 117 of the Treasury Department Appropriations Act for Fiscal Year 1999 also mandated that the State and Treasury Departments "shall fully, promptly, and effectively assist" any judgment creditor or court issuing a judgment against a terrorist State "in identifying, locating, and executing against the property of that foreign state.. .." [34] Because of the Administration's continuing objections, however, section 117 also gave the President authority to "waive the requirements of this section in the interest of national security." On October 21, 1998, President Clinton signed the legislation into law and immediately executed the waiver. [35] The President explained his reasons in the signing statement for the bill as follows:

> I am concerned about section 117 of the Treasury/General Government appropriations section of the act, which amends the Foreign Sovereign Immunities Act. If this section were to result in attachment and execution against foreign embassy properties, it would encroach on my authority under the Constitution to "receive Ambassadors and other public ministers." Moreover, if applied to foreign diplomatic or consular property, section 117 would place the United States in breach of its international treaty obligations. It would put at risk the protection we enjoy at every embassy and consulate throughout the world by eroding the principle that diplomatic property must be protected regardless of bilateral relations. Absent my authority to waive section 117's attachment provision, it would also effectively eliminate use of blocked assets of terrorist States in the national security interests of the United States, including denying an important source of leverage. In addition, section 117 could seriously impair our ability to enter into global claims settlements that are fair to all U.S. claimants, and could result in U.S. taxpayer liability in the event of a contrary claims tribunal judgment. To the extent possible, I shall construe section 117 in a manner consistent with my constitutional authority and with U.S. international legal obligations, and for the above reasons, I have exercised the waiver authority in the national security interest of the United States. [36]

106th Congress: Enactment of § 2002 of the Victims of Trafficking and Violence Protection Act of 2000 (VTVPA)

President Clinton's exercise of the waiver authority conferred by section 117 of the FY1999 Treasury Department appropriations act blocked those with default judgments against Cuba and Iran from attaching the diplomatic property and frozen assets of those States to satisfy the judgments. [37] In response, various Members during the 106th Congress pressed for additional amendments to the FSIA that would override the President's waiver of section 117 and allow the judgments against terrorist States to be satisfied out of the States' frozen assets. Congress held hearings to consider the Justice for Victims of Terrorism Act, [38] which was adopted as revised by the House and reported in the Senate. The Clinton Administration opposed the measure, and it was not enacted into law. Instead, negotiations with the Administration led by Senators Lautenberg and Mack resulted in the enactment of section 2002 of the Victims of Trafficking and Violence Against Women Act of 2000, [39] which created an alternative compensation system for some judgment holders. It mandated the payment of a portion of the damages awarded in the Alejandre judgment out of Cuba's frozen assets and a portion of ten designated judgments against Iran out of U.S. appropriated funds "not otherwise obligated." In the meantime, additional and substantial default judgments continued to be handed down in other suits against Iran [40]; and a number of new suits against terrorist States were filed. [41]

Like § 117 of the Fiscal 1999 Appropriations Act for the Treasury Department, the Justice for Victims of Terrorism Act would have amended the FSIA to allow the attachment of all of the assets of a terrorist State, including its blocked assets, its diplomatic and consular properties, and moneys due from or payable by the United States. To that end it would have repealed the waiver authority granted in § 117 and allowed the President to waive the authorization to attach assets only with respect to the premises of a foreign diplomatic or consular mission.

In hearings on the measure, the Clinton Administration was repeatedly criticized for its opposition to the efforts of victims of terrorism to collect on the judgments they had obtained. Senator Mack, cosponsor of the Justice for Victims of Terrorism Act in the Senate, stated:

> ... Mr. Chairman, the President made promises to the families, encouraged them to seek justice, calling their efforts brave and courageous. He pledged to fight terrorism and signed several laws supporting the rights of victims to take terrorists to court. But ultimately, he has chosen to protect terrorist assets over

the rights of American citizens seeking justice. This is simply not what America stands for. Victims' families must know that the U.S. Government stands with them in actions, as well as words. [42]

Several of the victims' relatives also made statements criticizing the Administration's actions. [43]

Treasury Deputy Secretary Stuart E. Eizenstat, Defense Department Under Secretary for Policy Walter Slocombe, and State Department Under Secretary for Policy Thomas Pickering responded for the Administration in a joint statement. [44] While expressing support for the goal of "finding fair and just compensation for [the] grievous losses and unimaginable experiences" of the victims of terrorism, they said that the Victims of Terrorism Act was "fundamentally flawed" and had "five principal negative effects," as follows:

> First, blocking of assets of terrorist States is one of the most significant economic sanctions tools available to the President. The proposed legislation would undermine the President's ability to combat international terrorism and other threats to national security by permitting the wholesale attachment of blocked property, thereby depleting the pool of blocked assets and depriving the U.S. of a source of leverage in ongoing and office (sic) sanctions programs, such as was used to gain the release of our citizens held hostage in Iran in 1981 or in gaining information about POW's and MIA's as part of the normalization process with Vietnam.
>
> Second, it would cause the U.S. to violate its international treaty obligations to protect and respect the immunity of diplomatic and consular property of other nations, and would put our own diplomatic and consular property around the world at risk of copycat attachment, with all that such implies for the ability of the United States to conduct diplomatic and consular relations and protect personnel and facilities.
>
> Third, it would create a race to the courthouse benefiting one small, though deserving, group of Americans over a far larger group of deserving Americans. For example, in the case of Cuba, many Americans have waited decades to be compensated for both the loss of property and the loss of the lives of their loved ones. This would leave no assets for their claims and others that may follow. Even with regard to current judgment holders, it would result in their competing for the same limited pool of assets, which would be exhausted very quickly and might not be sufficient to satisfy all judgments.
>
> Fourth, it would breach the long-standing principle that the United States Government has sovereign immunity from attachment, thereby preventing the U.S. Government from making good on its debts and international obligations and potentially causing the U.S. taxpayer to incur substantial financial liability, rather than achieving the stated goal of forcing Iran to bear the burden of paying

these judgments. The Congressional Budget Office ("CBO") has recognized this by scoring the legislation at $420 million, the bulk of which is associated with the Foreign Military Sales ("FMS") Trust Fund. Such a waiver of sovereign immunity would expose the Trust Fund to writs of attachment, which would inject an unprecedented and major element of uncertainty and unreliability into the FMS program by creating an exception to the processes and principles under which the program operates.

Fifth, it would direct courts to ignore the separate legal status of States and their agencies and instrumentalities, overturning Supreme Court precedent and basic principles of corporate law and international practice by making state majority-owned corporations liable for the debts of the state and establishing a dangerous precedent for government owned enterprises like the U.S. Overseas Private Investment Corporation ("OPIC").

Notwithstanding these contentions, the Senate and House Judiciary Committees reported, and the House passed, a slightly amended version of the Justice for Victims of Terrorism Act. The bill in the Senate was reported without a committee report. The House Judiciary Committee stated in its report:

> The President's continued use of his waiver power has frustrated the legitimate rights of victims of terrorism, and thus this legislation is required. While still allowing the President to block the attachment of embassies and necessary operating assets, H.R. 3485 would amend the law to specifically deny blockage of attachment of proceeds from any property which has been used for any non- diplomatic purpose or proceeds from any asset which is sold or transferred for value to a third party. [45]

The House passed the bill by voice vote under a suspension of the rules. [46]

The Clinton Administration persisted in opposing the bill, however, and that led to extensive negotiations between the Administration and interested Members of Congress. Ultimately, these negotiations led to the addition to an unrelated bill pending in conference of a limited alternative compensation scheme, which was signed into law by President Clinton on October 28, 2000. [47] Section 2002 of the Victims of Trafficking and Violence Protection Act of 2000 directed the Secretary of the Treasury to pay portions of any judgments against Cuba and Iran that had been handed down by July 20, 2002, or that would be handed down in any suits that had been filed on one of five named dates on or before July 27, 2000. The judgments that had been handed down by July 20, 2000, were the Alejandre, Flatow, Cicippio, Anderson and Eisenfeld cases. Six suits had been filed against Iran on the five dates specified in the statute — February 17, 1999;

June 7, 1999; January 28, 2000; March 15, 2000; and July 27, 2000 — and all have subsequently been decided. [48] (See Appendix A for a full list of the cases.) Section 2002 gave the claimants in these eleven suits three options:

- First, they could obtain from the Treasury Department 110 percent of the compensatory damages awarded in their judgments, plus interest, if they agreed to relinquish all rights to collect further compensatory and punitive damages;
- Second, they could receive 100 percent of the compensatory damages awarded in their judgments, plus interest, if they agreed to relinquish (a) all rights to further compensatory damages awarded by U.S. courts and (b) all rights to attach certain categories of property in satisfaction of their judgments for punitive damages, including Iran's diplomatic and consular property as well as property that is at issue in claims against the United States before an international tribunal. The property in the latter category included Iran's Foreign Military Sales (FMS) trust fund, which remains at issue in a case before the Iran-U.S. Claims Tribunal.
- Third, claimants could decline to obtain any payments from the Treasury Department and continue to pursue satisfaction of their judgments as best they could. [49]

To pay a portion of the judgment against Cuba in the Alejandre case, the statute directed that the President vest and liquidate Cuban government properties that have been frozen under TWEA. For the ten designated cases against Iran, § 2002 provided for payment out of U.S. funds, as follows:

- The statute directed the Secretary of the Treasury to use any proceeds that have accrued from the rental of Iranian diplomatic and consular property in the United States plus appropriated funds not otherwise obligated (meaning U.S. funds) up to the amount contained in Iran's Foreign Military Sales account. The Foreign Military Sales (FMS) Fund [50] had, as of 2000, about $377 million in funds. The account originally contained funds deposited by Iran to pay for military equipment and services during the reign of the Shah. However, Congress also provided funds for the account in order to continue to pay contractors for goods and services after Iran terminated contracts under the FMS program. [51] Disposition of military equipment procured for Iran through the FMS fund and the money remaining in the FMS account is an unresolved issue between the United States and Iran before the U.S.-Iran Claims Tribunal, where Iran has filed claims seeking billions of dollars primarily for alleged overcharges and nondeliveries of military equipment, as well as for allegedly unjustified charges billed to Iran for terminating its FMS program and the associated contracts. The United States has filed counterclaims to recover amounts it claims Iran owes on the contracts.

- For payments paid out of U.S. funds, § 2002 stated that the United States would be subrogated to the rights of the persons paid (meaning that the United States would be entitled to pursue their right to payment of the damage awards from Iran).
- Section 2002 further provided that the United States "shall pursue" these subrogated rights as claims or offsets to any claims or awards that Iran may have against the United States; and it bars the payment or release of any funds to Iran from frozen assets or from the Foreign Military Sales Fund until these subrogated claims have been satisfied.

Section 2002 further expressed the "sense of the Congress" that relations between the United States and Iran should not be normalized until these subrogated claims have been "dealt with to the satisfaction of the United States." It also "reaffirmed the President's statutory authority to manage and ... vest foreign assets located in the United States for the purpose[] ... of assisting and, where appropriate, making payments to victims of terrorism." In addition, § 2002 modified one provision of § 117 of the Treasury Department appropriations act for fiscal 1999 by changing the mandate that the State and Treasury Departments "shall" assist those who have obtained judgments against terrorist States in locating the assets of those States to the more permissive "should make every effort" to assist such judgment creditors.

Finally, § 2002 modified the waiver authority that the President had been given in § 117. It repealed that subsection and instead provided that "[t]he President may waive any provision of paragraph (1) in the interest of national security." (Paragraph (1) was the subsection that allowed the frozen assets of a terrorist State, including its diplomatic property, to be attached in satisfaction of a judgment against that State.) [52]

Immediately after signing the legislation into law on October 28, 2000, President Clinton exercised the substitute waiver authority granted by § 2002 and waived "subsection (f)(1) of section 1610 of title 28, United States Code, in the interest of national security." [53] Thus, except to the extent § 2002 allowed the blocked assets of Cuba to be used to satisfy a portion of the Alejandre judgment, it did not eliminate the bar to the attachment of the diplomatic property and the blocked assets of terrorist States to satisfy judgments against those States. [54]

In November and December 2000, the Office of Foreign Assets Control in the Department of the Treasury issued a notice detailing the procedures governing application for payment by those in the eleven designated cases who might want to obtain the partial payment of their judgments afforded by § 2002. [55] All of the claimants in the designated suits chose to obtain such compensation.

In early 2001 the federal government liquidated $96.7 million of the $193.5 million of Cuban assets that had previously been blocked and paid that amount to the claimants in the Alejandre suit and their attorneys. [56] The claimants in the ten designated cases against Iran variously chose to receive either 100 percent or 110 percent of their compensatory damages awards; and they ultimately received more than $380 million in compensation out of U.S. funds. (See Appendix A for a listing of the cases, the payments made, and the option chosen.)

107th Congress: Additional Cases Added to § 2002 and Attachment of Assets Allowed in Other Cases

Subsequent to the enactment of § 2002 of the Victims of Trafficking statute in late 2000, the courts handed down additional default judgments in suits against terrorist States under the FSIA exception. As noted above, six of these additional judgments were covered by the compensation scheme set forth in § 2002 because the suits had been filed on one of the five dates on or prior to July 27, 2000 specified in the statute. [57] But other default judgments, [58] as well as additional cases that were filed and remained pending, were not covered by § 2002. As a consequence, pressure for finding some means to compensate the additional claimants continued to grow. [59] The 107th Congress enacted several pieces of legislation, as follows:

(1) Directive to develop a comprehensive compensation scheme (P.L. 107-77). In the Act Making Appropriations for the Departments of Commerce, Justice, and State, the Judiciary, and Related Agencies for the Fiscal Year Ending September 30, 2002, [60] Congress in November 2001 directed President Bush to submit, no later than the time he submitted the proposed budget for FY2003,

> a legislative proposal to establish a comprehensive program to ensure fair, equitable, and prompt compensation for all United States victims of international terrorism (or relatives of deceased United States victims of international terrorism) that occurred or occurs on or after November 1, 1979. [61]

That directive had not been part of either the House or Senate-passed versions of H.R. 2500. But it was added in lieu of an amendment sponsored by Senator Hollings that the Senate had adopted, without debate, which would have authorized partial payment of the judgments in five additional cases (including the Roeder case, infra). [62] In explaining the conference substitute for that provision, the conference report stated:

> Objections from all quarters have been repeatedly raised against the current ad hoc approach to compensation for victims of international terrorism. Objections and concerns, however, will no longer suffice. It is imperative that the Secretary of State, in coordination with the Departments of Justice and Treasury and other relevant agencies, develop a legislative proposal that will provide fair and prompt compensation to all U.S. victims of international terrorism. A compensation system already is in place for the victims of the September 11 terrorist attacks; a similar system should be available to victims of international terrorism. [63]

In signing the measure into law, President Bush cited the directive regarding submission of a comprehensive plan and stated that "I will apply this provision consistent with my constitutional responsibilities." [64] No such plan was put forward in the second session of the 107th Congress.

(2) Coverage of additional cases under § 2002 (P.L. 107-228). On September 30, 2002, President Bush signed into law a measure — the Foreign Relations Authorization Act for Fiscal 2003 — that added cases filed against Iran on June 6, 2000, and January 16, 2002 to those that can be compensated under § 2002. [65] The first case — Carlson v. The Islamic Republic of Iran [66] — was by six Navy divers who were on board a TWA airliner that was hijacked in 1985 and who were subsequently imprisoned and tortured by Lebanese Shiite terrorists. That suit had been filed separately from a suit by the family of Robert Stethem, who was murdered in the course of the same hijacking — Stethem v. The Islamic Republic of Iran. [67] But the two suits had been consolidated for trial, and the court decided the cases together. [68] Stethem's suit had been included as one of the cases that was compensable under § 2002 as originally enacted, but the companion suit by the Navy divers had not been included. The amendment enacted into law as part of the foreign relations authorization bill had been adopted by the House on May 16, 2001, by voice vote to rectify what its sponsor termed this "inadvertent error." [69] The second case, specified by its filing date of January 16, 2002, was added to the measure by the conference committee and was identified by the Office of Foreign Assets Control as the case of Kapar v. Islamic Republic of Iran.

(3) Attachment of frozen assets authorized (P.L. 107-297). On November 26, 2002, President Bush signed the Terrorism Risk Insurance Act (TRIA) into law. [70] Section 201 of TRIA overrode long-standing objections by the Clinton and Bush Administrations to make the frozen assets of terrorist States available to satisfy judgments for compensatory damages against such States (and organizations and persons) as follows:

> Notwithstanding any other provision of law, and except as provided in subsection (b), in every case in which a person has obtained a judgment against a terrorist party on a claim based upon an act of terrorism, or for which a terrorist party is not immune under section 1605(a)(7) of title 28, United States Code, the blocked assets of that terrorist party (including the blocked assets of any agency or instrumentality of that terrorist party) shall be subject to execution or attachment in aid of execution in order to satisfy such judgment to the extent of any compensatory damages for which such terrorist party has been adjudged liable. [71]

Subsection (b) of § 201, in turn, narrowed the waiver authority previously afforded the President on this subject and permits the President to waive this provision "in the national security interest" only with respect to "property subject to the Vienna Convention on Diplomatic Relations or the Vienna Convention on Consular Relations."

In addition, § 201 of P.L. 107-297 amended § 2002 of the Victims of Trafficking Act with respect to suits against Iran:

- It added to the list of suits against Iran that are compensable under § 2002, without further identification, all those that were filed before October 28, 2000.
- It made 90 percent of the amount remaining in the § 2002 fund (about $15.7 million) available to pay the compensatory damages awarded in any judgment rendered in the cases previously added by P.L. 107-228 and by this statute which had been entered as of the date of this statute's enactment (November 26, 2002) and provided that, if the total amount of damages awarded exceeded the amount available, each claimant is to receive a proportionate amount. [72]
- It set aside the remaining 10 percent of the § 2002 fund for compensation under the same formula of the final judgment entered in the case filed against Iran on January 16, 2002 (Kapar v. Islamic Republic of Iran).

- It provided that persons who receive less than 100 percent of the compensatory damages awarded in their judgments against Iran under the foregoing scheme do not have to relinquish their right to obtain additional compensatory damages, as was required of those previously compensated under § 2002, but only to relinquish their right to obtain punitive damages.

Bush Administration's Proposed Compensation Alternative

During the 108th Congress, Senator Lugar (R-IN) introduced an Administration proposal that would have established an administrative procedure to provide compensation to victims of international terrorism as an alternative to suits under the terrorist State exception to the FSIA. S. 1275 would have amended § 201 of the Terrorism Risk Insurance Act to provide that claimants who obtain judgments against terrorist States after the date of the bill's introduction could no longer collect on the compensatory damages portions of those judgments out of the States' blocked assets. As an alternative, the bill would have created a new compensation scheme called the "Benefits for Victims of International Terrorism Program." Administered by the State Department, the program would have been able to authorize the payment of up to $262,000 to those who have been killed, injured, or held hostage by an act of international terrorism. [73] A person who accepted benefits under the program would have been barred from bringing or maintaining a suit against a terrorist State for the same act.

In a hearing on the bill by the Senate Committee on Foreign Relations on July 17, 2003, [74] William Taft, then State Department Legal Adviser, asserted that "[t]he current litigation-based system of compensation is inequitable, unpredictable, occasionally costly to the U.S. taxpayer, and damaging to foreign policy and national security goals of this country." Stuart Eizenstat, now in private practice but formerly the Clinton Administration's point man on this issue, claimed that the amount of compensation that would be provided under the bill was insufficient to make the scheme a viable alternative to litigation. Allan Gerson, a professor and trial lawyer involved in suits under the FSIA exception, charged that the proposal would deny plaintiffs their day in court and do nothing to hold terrorist States accountable for their actions. No further action was taken on the bill.

THE SEARCH FOR A CAUSE OF ACTION: CICIPPIO-PULEO V. IRAN

After Congress passed the Flatow Amendment in 1996, providing for a cause of action against foreign officials for terrorist conduct, the judge in the Flatow case held Iran itself liable under a theory of respondeat superior, and awarded compensatory as well as punitive damages. [75] Many trial courts followed the Flatow precedent, awarding both compensatory and punitive damages against a foreign State despite the textual limitations in the FSIA exception with respect to punitive damages. [76] However, the Court of Appeals for the District of Columbia held in 2004 that the amendment does not provide a cause of action against terrorist States themselves, [77] including governmental agencies and separate commercial "agencies and instrumentalities" under the FSIA. [78] Moreover, although the Flatow Amendment created a cause of action against an "official, employee, or agent of a [designated terrorist State] while acting within the scope of his or her office, employment, or agency," the court held that it did not create a cause of action against foreign officials in their official capacities. [79]

The Cicippio-Puleo case involved claims for damages brought by the adult children and siblings of Joseph Cicippio, a hostage victim who had previously won a $30 million default judgment against Iran for financing the Hezbollah terrorists who kidnapped him in Beirut and held him hostage there for some five years. [80] The children and siblings had not participated in the original lawsuit, but filed suit in 2001 for intentional infliction of emotional distress and the loss of solatium they suffered as a result of Mr. Cicippio' s ordeal. The district court judge dismissed the case for failure to state a claim upon which relief could be granted, holding that the prevailing common law rule governing third party claims for outrageous conduct causing severe emotional distress prevented plaintiffs' recovery. [81] The appellate court requested a briefing from the U.S. government explaining its interpretation of the relevant statutes, and, at the government's urging, [82] held that neither the FSIA exception nor the Flatow Amendment created a cause of action against a foreign State. The court remanded the case to the district court to permit the plaintiffs to amend their complaint to state a valid cause of action. On remand, the judge awarded the plaintiffs $91 million in compensatory damages for intentional infliction of emotional distress under Pennsylvania law. [83]

With respect to lawsuits against individual officials and employees of foreign governments, the court agreed with the U.S. government that "insofar as the

Flatow Amendment creates a private right of action against officials, employees, and agents of foreign states, the cause of action is limited to claims against those officials in their individual, as opposed to their official, capacities." [84] This interpretation was said to follow from Supreme Court holdings establishing that an official-capacity claim against a government official is in substance a claim against the government itself, inasmuch as the government would be responsible to pay any damages awarded against its officials. [85] Nevertheless, some judges have continued to award punitive damages against foreign officials acting in their official capacity. [86] Some judges have found foreign officials liable in their personal capacities, awarding treble damages against those officials under the Antiterrorism Act (ATA), 18 U.S.C. § 2333 (despite the limitation in 18 U.S.C. § 2337 making that cause of action unavailable against U.S. and foreign officials "acting within his or her official capacity or under color of legal authority"). [87]

The Cicippio-Puleo ruling complicated plaintiffs' efforts to sue designated State sponsors of terrorism by requiring them to identify a source of law outside the FSIA to provide a substantive cause of action. Some plaintiffs who had already been awarded default judgments were obliged to amend their complaints to identify a basis for liability. [88] Plaintiffs have, with a few exceptions, had little difficulty establishing a cause of action under various U.S. state laws without relying on the Flatow Amendment. However, the application of state tort law has resulted in some disparity in the availability or amount of damages to which plaintiffs may be entitled. For example, in one case, damages for intentional infliction of emotional distress were denied to plaintiffs domiciled in Pennsylvania and Louisiana because those states' tort laws impose a presence requirement for third party plaintiffs to recover for emotional distress. [89] The application of federal statutes outside the FSIA has also resulted in a lower amount of damages than might have been awarded under earlier court interpretations of the Flatow Amendment. [90] Plaintiffs suing for damages related to the terrorist attack on the U.S.S. Cole in 2000 were awarded a cumulative sum less than $8 million for economic damages, and were not entitled to damages for pain and suffering, because the judge found the Death on the High Seas Act [91] to provide the only remedy.

IRAN HOSTAGES CASE:
ROEDER V. ISLAMIC REPUBLIC OF IRAN

Judicial Proceedings

In late 2000 a suit was filed in federal district court on behalf of the 52 embassy staffers who had been held hostage by Iran from 1979-8 1 and on behalf of their families. Roeder v. Islamic Republic of Iran [92] sought both compensatory and punitive damages from Iran. In August of 2001, the trial court granted a default judgment to the plaintiffs and scheduled a hearing on the damages to be awarded.

But in October 2001, a few days before the scheduled hearing, the U.S. government intervened in the proceeding and moved that the judgment be vacated and the case dismissed. The government contended that the suit did not meet all of the requirements of the terrorist State exception to the FSIA (notably, that Iran had not been designated as a State sponsor of terrorism at the time the U.S. personnel were held hostage) and that the suit was barred by the explicit provisions of the 1981 Algiers Accords that led to the release of the hostages. [93]

While that motion was pending before the court, Congress passed as part of the Hollings amendment to the FY2002 Appropriations Act for the Departments of Commerce, Justice, and State a provision specifying that Roeder should be deemed to be included within the terrorist State exception to the FSIA. As amended, the pertinent section of the FSIA excludes suits against terrorist States from the immunity generally accorded foreign States but directs the courts to decline to hear such a case (with the amendment in italics)

> if the foreign state was not designated as a state sponsor of terrorism ... at the time the act occurred, unless later so designated as a result of such act or the act is related to Case Number 1:00CV03110 (ESG) in the United States District Court for the District of Columbia. [94]

The conference report on the bill explained the provision as follows:

> Subsection (c) quashes the State Department's motion to vacate the judgment obtained by plaintiffs in Case Number 1 :00CV03 110 (ESG) in the United States District Court for the District of Columbia. Consistent with current law, subsection (c) does not require the United States government to make any payments to satisfy the judgment. [95]

In signing the appropriations act into law on November 28, 2001, however, President Bush took note of this provision and commented as follows:

> [S]ubsection (c) ... purports to remove Iran's immunity from suit in a case brought by the 1979 Tehran hostages in the District Court for the District of Columbia. To the maximum extent permitted by applicable law, the executive branch will act, and will encourage the courts to act, with regard to subsection 626(c) of the Act in a manner consistent with the obligations of the United States under the Algiers Accord that achieved the release of U.S. hostages in 1981. [96]

The government continued to pursue its motion to dismiss the case, arguing, inter alia, that the suit is barred by the Algiers Accords. During the course of the proceeding Judge Sullivan expressed concern regarding the lack of clarity of the recent Congressional enactment with respect to that contention. A week later in the fiscal 2002 appropriations act for the Department of Defense, the 107th Congress included a provision making a minor technical correction in the reference to the Roeder case. [97] But the conference report also elaborated on what it said was the effect and intent of the earlier amendment of the FSIA with respect to Roeder, seemingly in response to Judge Sullivan's expression of concern. The conference report explained that:

> The language included in Section 626(c) of Public Law 107-77 quashed the Department of State's motion to vacate the judgment obtained by plaintiffs in Case Number 1 :00CV03 1 10(EGS) and reaffirmed the validity of this claim and its retroactive application.... The provision included in Section 626(c) of Public Law 107-77 acknowledges that, notwithstanding any other authority, the American citizens who were taken hostage by the Islamic Republic of Iran in 1979 have a claim against Iran under the Antiterrorism Act of 1996 and the provision specifically allows the judgment to stand for purposes of award damages consistent with Section 2002 of the Victims of Terrorism Act of 2000 (Public Law 106-386, 114 Stat. 1541). [98]

Nonetheless, in signing the Department of Defense appropriations measure into law on January 10, 2002, President Bush continued to insist as follows:

> Section 208 of Division B makes a technical correction to subsection 626(c) of Public Law 107-77 (the FY2002 Commerce, Justice, State, the Judiciary and Related Agencies Appropriations Act), but does nothing to alter the effect of that provision or any other provision of law. Since the enactment of sub-section 626(c) and consistent with it, the executive branch has encouraged the courts to act, and will continue to encourage the courts to act, in a manner consistent with

the obligations of the United States under the Algiers Accords that achieved the release of U.S. hostages in 1981. [99]

After two additional hearings, Judge Sullivan on April 18, 2002, granted the government's motion to vacate the default judgment against Iran and to dismiss the suit. [100] In a lengthy opinion the court concluded that:

- at the time it entered a default judgment for plaintiffs on August 17, 2001, it did not, in fact, have jurisdiction over the case and, thus, should not have entered a judgment [101];
- the cause of action which Congress had adopted in late 1996 did not, in fact, apply to suits against terrorist States but only against the officials, employees, and agents of those States who perpetrate terrorist acts [102]; and
- the provision of the Algiers Accords committing the United States to bar suits against Iran for the incident constitutes the substantive law of the case, and Congress's two enactments specifically concerning the case were too ambiguous to conclude that it specifically intended to override this international commitment. [103]

In addition, the court in dicta suggested that Congress's enactments on the Roeder case might have interfered with its adjudication of the case in a manner that raised constitutional separation of powers concerns. [104] It also chastised the plaintiffs' attorneys for what it said were serious breaches of their professional and ethical responsibilities. [105]

The U.S. Court of Appeals for the District of Columbia affirmed the decision of the lower court, placing emphasis on the fact that the legislative history plaintiffs sought to use — the joint explanatory statement prepared by House and Senate conferees — is not part of the Conference Report voted on by both houses of Congress and thus does not carry the force of law. [106]

> Executive agreements are essentially contracts between nations, and like contracts between individuals, executive agreements are expected to be honored by the parties. Congress (or the President acting alone) may abrogate an executive agreement, but legislation must be clear to ensure that Congress - and the President - have considered the consequences. The "requirement of clear statement assures that the legislature has in fact faced, and intended to bring into issue, the critical matters involved in the judicial decision." The kind of legislative history offered here cannot repeal an executive agreement when the legislation itself is silent. [Citations omitted].

The court denied that its interpretation rendered any act of Congress futile. On the contrary, it stated that, "[i]f constitutional ... the amendments had the effect of removing Iran's sovereign immunity, which the United States had raised in its motion to vacate." [107]

Efforts to Abrogate the Algiers Accords

Subsequent to the trial court's decision in Roeder, efforts have been made in the 107th, the 108th, and the 109th Congresses to enact legislation that would explicitly abrogate the provision of the Algiers Accords barring the hostages' suit. On July 24, 2002, the Senate Appropriations Committee reported the "Fiscal 2003 Appropriations Act for the Departments of Commerce, Justice, and State" (S. 2778). Section 616 of that bill proposed to amend the FSIA as follows:

> SEC. 616. Section 1605 of title 28, United States Code is amended by adding a new subsection (h) as follows:
> (h) CAUSE OF ACTION FOR IRANIAN HOSTAGES- Notwithstanding any provision of the Algiers Accords, or any other international agreement, any United States citizen held hostage in Iran after November 1, 1979, and their spouses and children at the time, shall have a claim for money damages against the government of Iran. Any provision in an international agreement, including the Algiers Accords that purports to bar such suit is abrogated. This subsection shall apply retroactively to any cause of action cited in 28 U.S.C. 1605(a)(7)(A).

In explaining the provision, the report of the Committee simply stated that "Section 616 clarifies section 626 of Public Law 107-77 that the Algiers Accord is abrogated for the purposes of providing a cause of action for the Iranian hostages." [108] The measure received no further action prior to the adjournment of the 107th Congress, however.

In the 1 08th Congress the Senate added amendments to three appropriations bills that expressly would have abrogated the Algiers Accord, but in each case the amendment was deleted in conference. [109] The 109th Congress did not take up any legislation to abrogate the Algiers Accords. One bill, H.R. 3358, would have declared the Algiers Accords abrogated and inapplicable, and would have directed the Secretary of the Treasury to pay the Roeder plaintiffs $1,000 per day of captivity (family members were to be awarded $500 per day of captivity of the hostages), to be paid out of the FMS fund and frozen assets belonging to Iran. No action was taken on the bill, but it has been re-introduced in the 1 10th Congress as H.R. 394. In addition, H.R. 6305/S. 3878 would have provided up to $500,000 for victims of hostage-taking, including specifically the Iran hostages and family members named in the Roeder case, who would have been eligible for additional compensation from the FMS account. The bill did not mention the Algiers Accords, and it would have prohibited recipients from commencing or maintaining a civil action in U.S. court against a foreign State. However, payment of compensation out of Iran's FMS fund could arguably violate the Algiers Accords in the event the U.S.-Iran Claims Tribunal finds that those funds are the property of Iran. Similar legislation has been introduced in the 110th Congress as H.R. 3369 and H.R. 3346 (see infra).

In creating a federal cause of action against terrorist States (P.L. 110-181, codified at 28 U.S.C. § 1605A, see infra), the 110th Congress carried over the language from former 28 U.S.C. § 1605(a)(7) that conferred jurisdiction over the Roeder case, despite the fact that the case has been dismissed. Nothing in the statute expressly abrogates the Algiers Accords, however, making it unlikely that the Roeder plaintiffs will prevail in an effort to sue Iran under the new cause of action.

IRAQ: LAWSUITS INVOLVING ACTS OF SADDAM HUSSEIN REGIME

Confiscation of Blocked Assets for Reconstruction

On March 20, 2003, immediately after the U.S. and its coalition partners initiated military action against Iraq, President Bush issued an executive order providing for the confiscation and vesting of Iraq's frozen assets in the U.S. government and placing them in the Development Fund for Iraq for use in the postwar reconstruction of Iraq. [110] According to the Terrorist Assets Report 2002 published by the Office of Foreign Assets Control, Iraq's blocked assets totaled approximately $1.73 billion at the end of 2002. However, the President's order excluded from confiscation Iraq's diplomatic and consular property as well as assets that had, prior to March 20, 2003, been ordered attached in satisfaction of judgments against Iraq rendered pursuant to the terrorist suit provision of the FSIA and § 201 of the Terrorism Risk Insurance Act (which reportedly total about $300 million). [111] The President stated that the remaining assets "should be used to assist the Iraqi people...." Thus, notwithstanding the enactment of § 201 of TRIA, the President's action made Iraq's frozen assets unavailable to those who, after March 20, 2003, obtained judgments against that State for its sponsorship of, or complicity in, acts of terrorism.

Subsequently, the President took several additional actions complementing and reinforcing this executive order. In the Emergency Wartime Supplemental Appropriations Act for Fiscal 2003 ("EWSAA"), Congress provided that "the President may make inapplicable with respect to Iraq section 620A of the Foreign Assistance Act of 1961 or any other provision of law that applies to countries that have supported terrorism." [112] On the basis of that authority, President Bush on May 7, 2003, declared a number of provisions concerning terrorist States, including the FSIA exception and the section of the Terrorism Risk Insurance Act making their blocked assets available to victims of terrorism, inapplicable to Iraq. [113] On May 22, 2003, he issued another executive order providing that the Development Fund of Iraq cannot be attached or made subject to any other kind of judicial process. [114]

POW Lawsuit: Acree v. Republic of Iraq

Whether the President has the legal authority to restore Iraq's sovereign immunity and make its assets unavailable to victims of terrorism who had obtained judgments against Iraq was contested in Acree v. Republic of Iraq. [115] In that case a federal district court on July 7, 2003 — two and half months after the President's order — handed down a default judgment against Iraq for its imprisonment and torture of 17 American prisoners of war (POWs) during the first Gulf War in 1991. After detailing the treatment given the POWs, the court awarded them and their families $653 million in compensatory damages and added a punitive damages award of $306 million for the benefit of the POWs against Saddam Hussein and the Iraqi Intelligence Service. Upon request by the plaintiffs, Judge Roberts issued a temporary restraining order (TRO) requiring the government to retain at least $653 million of Iraq's assets vested in the United States by President Bush's executive order pending further decision by the court.

The Justice Department then sought to intervene in the case, arguing that Iraq's sovereign immunity had been restored by Presidential Determination pursuant to authority granted by Congress. The court denied the government's motion to intervene as untimely because the Justice Department had waited 75 days past the Determination before it intervened, knowing that the Acree case was pending before the court. [116] Additionally, the court found that the government's interest in promoting a new, democratic Iraqi government did not constitute a cognizable interest warranting intervention as of right, especially absent any showing of how the default judgment impaired such interest. The court also held that only Iraq could assert a defense based on sovereign immunity, and that Congress and the President could not retroactively restore Iraq's previously waived sovereign immunity.

While the Presidential Determination did not retroactively restore Iraq's sovereign immunity, it was held effectively to preclude the plaintiffs from enforcing their judgment against the $1.73 billion in frozen Iraqi assets that had been vested by the President for the restoration of Iraq. [117] After an expedited hearing on the matter, the court on July 30, 2003, held that none of the assets in question could be attached by the plaintiffs; and the court dissolved the TRO. [118] In reaching that conclusion, the court relied primarily on the Supplemental Appropriations Act provision noted above and the subsequent actions by President Bush rather than on his March 20, 2003, executive order. The court concluded:

> The Act is Congressional authorization for the President to make TRIA prospectively inapplicable to Iraq, and the President exercised that authority when he issued the Determination on May 7, 2003. As a result, at the time the plaintiffs obtained their judgment against Iraq on July 7, 2003, TRIA was no longer an available mechanism for plaintiffs to use to satisfy their judgment. [119]

The Justice Department appealed the decision denying its motion to intervene, while plaintiffs appealed the decision that frozen Iraqi funds were unavailable to satisfy their judgment. The Court of Appeals for the D.C. Circuit held that the district court had abused its discretion by denying the government's motion to intervene. [120] However, the court reversed the President's Determination insofar as it nullified the FSIA provisions with respect to Iraq, finding that Congress had not intended to permit the President to revoke those provisions. The plaintiffs were nevertheless prevented from collecting, because the court of appeals vacated their judgment based on their failure to state a cause of action against Iraq, and because Saddam Hussein retained immunity for official conduct. The court followed its precedent in Cicippio-Puleo v. Islamic Republic of Iran [121] to hold that the terrorism exception to the FSIA combined with the Flatow Amendment, as in force at the time, created a private right of action against officials, employees and agents of a foreign government for their private conduct, but not against the foreign government itself, including its agencies and instrumentalities, or officials in their official capacity. [122] The Supreme Court declined to review the decision. [123] The Plaintiffs sought to reopen their case at the district court level in order to demonstrate the applicability of several causes of action. The district court, however, has dismissed the motion as moot, finding that the D.C. Circuit's earlier dismissal of their lawsuit without remanding it to the district court means that the court has no discretion to reopen it. [124]

Proposed Legislation: 108th and 109th Congresses

Two bills were introduced during the 108th Congress in the House of Representatives to provide relief for the plaintiffs. H.Con.Res. 344 would have expressed the sense of the Congress that the POWs and their immediate family members should be compensated for their suffering and injuries as the court had decided, notwithstanding § 1503 of EWSAA. The bill would also have expressed Congress's resolve to continue its oversight of the application of § 1503 "in order to ensure that it is not misinterpreted, including by divesting United States courts of jurisdiction, with respect the POWs and other victims of Iraqi terrorism." [125] Additionally, the Senate passed language in § 325 of its version of the Emergency Supplemental Appropriations for Iraq and Afghanistan Security and Reconstruction Act, 2004 (H.R. 3289), that would have found that

> the Attorney General should enter into negotiations with each such citizen, or the family of each such citizen, to develop a fair and reasonable method of providing compensation for the damages each such citizen incurred, including using assets of the regime of Saddam Hussein held by the Government of the United States or any other appropriate sources to provide such compensation.

The language was not enacted. [126]

The other House bill from the 108th Congress, H.R. 2224, the Prisoner of War Protection Act of 2003, would have allowed the plaintiffs, as well as any POWs who might later assert a cause of action in the more recent war against Iraq, to recover damages out of the $1.73 billion in frozen Iraqi assets that were vested by order of the President to pay for the reconstruction of Iraq.

Nothing similar to the Prisoner of War Protection Act was introduced in the 109th Congress, but H.Con.Res. 93 would have "express[ed] the sense of the Congress that the Department of Justice should halt efforts to block compensation for torture inflicted by the Government of Iraq on American prisoners of war during the 1991 Gulf War." H.R. 1321 proposed the payment of $1 million to each of the seventeen plaintiffs out of unobligated funds appropriated under the heading of "Iraq Relief and Reconstruction Fund" in the 2004 Emergency Supplemental. [127] Neither provision was enacted into law.

Other Cases Against Iraq

Smith v. Islamic Emirate of Afghanistan [128] was initially a lawsuit against Al Qaeda, Afghanistan, and the Taliban for damages related to the terrorist attacks on the World Trade Center in 2001. The plaintiffs subsequently amended their complaints to add Iraq and Saddam Hussein as defendants. None of the defendants entered an appearance. The complaint against Saddam Hussein was dismissed because the judge found it precluded by the Flatow Amendment provision excluding lawsuits against foreign officials in cases in which U.S. officials would not be liable for similar conduct. [129] The case against Iraq was permitted to continue, and the plaintiffs were found to have demonstrated to the court's satisfaction that Iraq had provided material support to Al Qaeda. [130] A final judgment was entered on July 14, 2003, awarding the plaintiffs approximately $104 million in compensatory damages, with Iraq deemed responsible for approximately $63.5 million of the total. By that time, however, the President had already vested Iraq's frozen funds in U.S. possession, which frustrated plaintiffs' efforts to satisfy their judgment under TRIA § 201. [131] The U.S. Court of Appeals for the 2d Circuit, in affirming the summary judgment in favor of the Federal Reserve Bank and the Treasury Department, found it unnecessary to rule on the validity of the President's order restoring Iraq's sovereign immunity, having found that the specific funds at issue were no longer blocked assets within the meaning of TRIA § 201. [132] Consequently, the judgment creditors in this case have not been prevented from seeking to satisfy their judgments from other assets. A similar case, O'Neill v. Republic of Iraq, Civil Action No. 1:04- 01076 (GBD) (D.D.C., filed February 10, 2004), remains pending.

Hill v. Republic of Iraq [133] began as a lawsuit against Iraq and Saddam Hussein by twelve U.S. citizens who were held in hostage status [134] by Iraq after its invasion of Kuwait in 1990. The former hostages, who were either held captive in or prevented from leaving Iraq or Kuwait from August 2 to mid-December of 1990, [135] and some of their families were awarded a cumulative $9 million in compensatory damages and $300 million in punitive damages in a default judgment. [136] The court subsequently found that an additional 168 plaintiffs had established their right to relief for being held hostage by Iraq; and the court awarded them approximately $85 million in compensatory damages.

[137] Judgment holders in this case were able to fully satisfy their compensatory judgments from Iraqi assets vested by the President in 2003. [138]

Vine v. Republic of Iraq [139] involves 237 plaintiffs who were unsuccessful in joining the Hill case after the judge denied class action status to the lawsuit and imposed a moratorium on the addition of new plaintiffs. The plaintiffs include U.S. nationals who were used as "human shields" by the Iraqi government to protect various strategic sites from attack, and any U.S. nationals in hiding in Iraq or Kuwait for fear of capture, [140] as well as some of their spouses. Iraq made an appearance in the case and moved to dismiss the claims on several grounds. The court dismissed causes of action based on the Flatow Amendment and federal common law, but permitted claims based on U.S. state and foreign law. The case remains pending.

The judge dismissed as untimely several other claims that had been consolidated with the Vine case for determining Iraq's motion to dismiss. Two journalists, Robert Simon, a CBS News reporter, and Roberto Alvarez, a cameraman working for CBS News, alleged that they were illegally seized and subsequently tortured by Iraqi officials in 199 1. [141] Nabil Seyam and others filed a separate action based similar allegations. [142] The court reasoned that the cause of action in these cases arose no later than December 1990, and that the 10-year statute of limitations had run prior to the cases' filings in 2003. Despite the statutory provision for "equitable tolling, including the period during which the foreign state was immune from suit," [143] the court determined that the four years between the passage of the terrorist exception to the FSIA and the deadline for filing within the statute of limitations was sufficient to preclude equitable tolling. [144] However, the Court of Appeals for the D.C. Circuit reversed that decision, holding that the statute of limitations under the statute did not run until 10 years after the enactment of the terrorism exception to the FSIA. [145]

Beaty v. Iraq [146] is a suit against Iraq by five children of two men who were held hostage in Iraq during the 1990s. The two hostages and their wives sued Iraq in 1996 in conjunction with several other former hostages and their spouses, Daliberti v.

Iraq, [147] and were able to recover the resulting default judgment from the Iraqi frozen funds vested by President Bush in 2003. The Beaty plaintiffs grounded their complaint on claims of intentional infliction of emotional distress under state common law, violations of customary international law incorporated into federal common law, and loss of solatium under federal common law. Iraq entered an appearance and moved to dismiss the complaint for failure to state a claim upon which relief can be granted, for grounds of nonjusticiability under the political question doctrine, and for lack of jurisdiction due to the presidential order relieving Iraq from the legal consequences of its status as a terrorist State. The court suggested its agreement with the government's position, expressed in several statements of interest filed in the case, that the presidential order validly restored Iraq's sovereign immunity and divested the court of jurisdiction [148]; however, the court was bound by the appellate court decision in Acree to hold that § 1503 of EWSAA did not authorize the President's efforts in that regard. The court rejected the plaintiffs' federal common law claims but permitted the suit to continue with respect to the state claims under Florida and Oklahoma law, and accepted that the facts established in the Daliberti case may be deemed established for the purposes of all further proceedings without further proof. Iraq's interlocutory appeal was unsuccessful, but it has filed a petition for certiorari at the Supreme Court regarding the validity of the President's order restoring Iraq's sovereign immunity pursuant to § 1503 of EWSAA. The Supreme Court has asked the Solicitor General for his views on whether to grant the petition. [149]

Lawton v. Republic of Iraq is a lawsuit against Iraq asserting damages based on the bombing of the Alfred P. Murrah Building in Oklahoma City in 1995. The plaintiffs allege that the bombing "was orchestrated, assisted technically and/or financially, and directly aided by agents" of the Republic of Iraq. [150] After Iraq failed to enter an appearance, the plaintiffs moved for a default judgment. The court initially denied the motion for failure to state a cause of action, but after the plaintiffs amended their complaint, the court entered a default against Iraq. Iraq subsequently entered an appearance and asked the court to set aside the entry of default, which the court granted based on its finding that Iraq had acted as expeditiously as possible, given the circumstances. The case remains pending.

Effect of FY2008 NDAA, § 1083 on Iraq and Cases Pending

Section 1083 of the National Defense Authorization Act for FY2008, P.L. 110-181 (discussed more fully infra) made numerous changes to the relevant FSIA terrorist State exceptions, including provisions to facilitate plaintiffs' efforts to attach defendant State assets in satisfaction of judgments and to enable plaintiffs (like those in the Acree case) whose claims were dismissed for lack of a federal cause of action to refile their claims under new 28 U.S.C. § 1605A (new FSIA terrorism exception and explicit cause of action against terrorist States). In addition, subsection (c)(4) of section 1083 states that section 1503 of the Emergency Wartime Supplemental Appropriations Act (EWSAA) (P.L. 108-11) "has [n]ever authorized, directly or indirectly, the making inapplicable of any provision of chapter 97 of title 28, United States Code, or the removal of the jurisdiction of any court of the United States." This provision would appear to be aimed at ensuring that no court construes section 1503 of EWSAA to restore Iraq's sovereign immunity with respect to actions involving terrorist acts that occurred while Iraq was designated a State sponsor of terrorism.

President Bush vetoed the first version of the FY2008 NDAA, H.R. 1585, on the stated basis that § 1083 would jeopardize Iraq's economic development and security. [151] In response, Congress passed H.R. 4986, virtually identical to the vetoed bill but authorizing the President to

> waive any provision of [§1083] with respect to Iraq, insofar as that provision may, in the President's determination, affect Iraq or any agency or instrumentality thereof, if the President determines that —the waiver is in the national security interest of the United States; the waiver will promote the reconstruction of, the consolidation of democracy in, and the relations of the United States with, Iraq; and Iraq continues to be a reliable ally of the United States and partner in combating acts of international terrorism. [152]

The waiver authority applies retroactively "regardless of whether, or the extent to which, the exercise of that authority affects any action filed before, on, or after the date of the exercise of that authority or of the enactment of [P.L. 110-181 (January 28, 2008)]." [153]

On the day the President signed the FY2008 NDAA into law, the White House signed a waiver [154] and issued a press release justifying the exercise of the waiver authority. [155] The memorandum declares that a waiver of all of the provisions of section 1083 with respect to Iraq "is in the national security interest of the United States," and lists the following factors:

- Absent a waiver, section 1083 would have a potentially devastating impact on Iraq's ability to use Iraqi funds to expand and equip the Iraqi Security Forces, which would have serious implications for U.S. troops in the field acting as part of the Multinational Force-Iraq and would harm anti-terrorism and counter-insurgency efforts.
- Application of section 1083 to Iraq or any agency or instrumentality thereof will hurt the interests of the United States by unacceptably interfering with political and economic progress in Iraq that is critically important to bringing U.S. troops home.
- If applied to Iraq or any agency or instrumentality thereof, the provisions of section 1083 would redirect financial resources from the continued reconstruction of Iraq and would harm Iraq's stability, contrary to the

interests of the United States. A waiver will ensure that Iraqi assets of the Central Bank of Iraq, the government and commercial entities in which Iraq has an interest, remain available to maintain macroeconomic stability in Iraq and support private sector development and trade.

- By providing for the maintenance of macroeconomic stability, the waiver of section 1083 will promote the consolidation of democracy in Iraq.
- Absent a waiver of section 1083, Iraq's ability to finance employment alternatives, vocational training, and job placement programs necessary to promote community reintegration and development efforts contributing to counterterrorism efforts would be harmed.
- By ensuring that Iraq and its agencies and instrumentalities are not subject to litigation or liability pursuant to section 1083, waiver of section 1083 will promote the close relationship between the United States and Iraq.

The waiver appears to foreclose any refiling of the Acree lawsuit under the new provision, but the D.C. Circuit's recent decision in Simon v. Republic of Iraq [156] may permit the Acree case to go forward as a case pending under previous 28 U.S.C. § 1605(a)(7), along with other pending claims against Iraq under the FSIA terrorism exception. [157] In Simon, Iraq argued that the repeal of § 1605(a)(7) cut off jurisdiction of pending cases, while the presidential waiver prevented their conversion into claims under new § 1605A. The court disagreed, interpreting § 1083(c) of the NDAA to repeal § 1605(a)(7) only as to future claims against State sponsors of terror. [158] Under this interpretation, plaintiffs with pending claims against defendants other than Iraq may be permitted to pursue claims under both the repealed § 1605(a)(7) and new § 1605A. The court also rejected Iraq's contention that the lawsuit should be dismissed as presenting a political question. Iraq will likely ask the Supreme Court to review the decision, possibly in conjunction with the Beaty case.

Final judgments against Iraq are not affected by the presidential waiver, but any judgments against Iraq will likely remain difficult to enforce. Some avenues available to plaintiffs to enforce terrorism judgments are not affected by § 1083, such as TRIA § 201 [159] and the non-terrorism related exceptions related to the property of a sovereign in 28 U.S.C. § 1610, [160] but these will likely remain unavailing with respect to Iraq because of the executive orders that vested the frozen assets and protect other assets from attachment by judgment creditors. [161] On the other hand, 28 U.S.C. § 1610(a)(7), revoking the immunity to attachment of foreign State property with respect to claims for which the foreign State is not immune under the terrorism exception to the FSIA (as it existed both prior to and as amended by the NDAA), might remain available against Iraq despite the waiver. [162] If that is the case, Iraqi government assets used for commercial purposes in the United States that are not subject to the protection of E.O. 13303 (which covers the Development Fund for Iraq and all interests associated with Iraqi petroleum and petroleum products), [163] would be subject to attachment and execution on valid terrorism judgments against Iraq. [164] The President could, however, issue another executive order to protect all Iraqi assets from attachment to satisfy judgments.

Possibly believing that pending cases would be dismissed due to the exercise of the waiver provision, Congress included in § 1083 its sense that

> [T]he President, acting through the Secretary of State, should work with the Government of Iraq on a state-to-state basis to ensure compensation for any meritorious claims based on terrorist acts committed by the Saddam Hussein regime against individuals who were United States nationals or members of the United States Armed Forces at the time of those terrorist acts and whose claims cannot be addressed in courts in the United States due to the exercise of the waiver authority [above]. [165]

MINISTRY OF DEFENSE (IRAN) V. ELAHI

Although Iran has not appeared in court to defend itself in any of the terrorism cases brought against it, it did nonetheless challenge a decision that allowed a judgment-holder to collect part of a judgment against Iran out of an award owed to Iran by a third party. [166] The Ministry of Defense and Support for the Armed Forces of the Islamic Republic of Iran (MOD) asked the Supreme Court to overturn a decision that allowed the respondent, Dariush Elahi to attach a $2.8 million arbitral award issued in Iran's favor by the International Chamber of Commerce for a breach of contract that occurred in 1979. Elahi had been awarded a default judgment of $311.7 million in a lawsuit against Iran and its Ministry of Intelligence and Security (MOIS) based on the 1990 the assassination of his brother, Dr. Cyrus Elahi, a dissident who was shot to death in Paris by agents of the Iranian intelligence service. [167] Dariush Elahi and another judgment-holder, Stephen Flatow, both attempted to intervene in MOD's suit against Cubic Defense Systems, Inc. to attach Iran's award in partial satisfaction of their judgments against Iran. Flatow's petition was denied after the court found that he had waived his right to attach such assets by accepting payment under section 2002 of the Victims of Trafficking and Violence Protection Act of 2000 (VTVPA). [168]

Elahi's lawsuit was one of those cases added later to section 2002 of the VTVPA, however; and since he was only able to collect a portion of the compensatory damages from U.S. funds, he retained the right to pursue satisfaction of the rest of the compensatory portion of his claim from Iranian blocked assets not at issue before the U.S.-Iran Claims Tribunal. Iran argued that its judgment retained immunity under the FSIA as military property. [169] The court rejected Iran's contention, noting that MOD did not assert that the judgment would be used for military purposes, but instead stated the money would be deposited in Iran's central bank. [170] The court also rejected Iran's contention that the judgment is protected as "the property ... of a foreign central bank or monetary authority held for its own account" within the meaning of section 1611(b)(1), because it found that language to apply only to money held by a foreign bank "to be used or held in connection with central banking activities." [171] MOD also sought to invoke the blocking regulations as a bar to the attachment of the judgment, but the court rejected that argument as well, pointing out that the transaction was permitted under a general license.

Finally, MOD sought to bring a collateral attack against Elahi's default judgment, contesting the jurisdiction of the court that issued it on the basis of the alleged invalidity of the FSIA terrorism exception under the Cicippio-Puleo decision, supra. The court, construing the jurisdictional question as one of personal jurisdiction rather than subject-matter jurisdiction, found that MOD could have attempted to void the judgment on this basis at the district court level, but had waited too long to raise the issue during collateral proceedings. Because MOD was unable to show that the district court that issued the default judgment in favor of Elahi acted in a manner inconsistent with due process, or that the district court lacked subject-matter jurisdiction over the case, the court affirmed the decision in favor of Elahi.

MOD petitioned for certiorari to the Supreme Court to review the decision on several bases. MOD challenged the Ninth Circuit's assumption that MOD is an "agency or instrumentality" of Iran rather than an integral part of the Iranian government without separate juridical status. This distinction has bearing under the FSIA as to how its assets are treated and whether it can be held liable for the debts of the Ministry of Intelligence and Security (MOIS). MOD also challenged the assessment that the judgment due it on a military contract is not military property under the FSIA. As to the collateral attack on Elahi's judgment, Iran argued that in the context of the FSIA, questions of personal jurisdiction and subject-matter jurisdiction over a foreign sovereign are so intimately linked as to be inseparable, which would allow MOD to dispute the validity of Elahi's default judgment by asserting it was founded on an invalid cause of action.

Based on the recommendation of the Solicitor General, the Supreme Court granted certiorari only with respect to the issue of MOD's status as an "agency or instrumentality" of Iran. In a per curiam opinion, the Court vacated the decision below on the grounds that MOD had not had an opportunity to present argument on the issue. [172] The Ninth Circuit had erred, according to the Court, because it had either mistakenly relied on a "concession" by the plaintiff that MOD was an "agency or instrumentality," or it had simply assumed that there was no relevant distinction between those entities and a foreign State proper. The FSIA provides an exception to the immunity from execution of the property of a foreign State only if such property is used for commercial purposes. By contrast, the property of an "agency or instrumentality" of a foreign State is not immune from execution if the entity is engaged in commercial activity in the United States, regardless of whether the property is used for the commercial activity. [173]

On remand, the appellate court found that MOD is a foreign State rather than an agency or instrumentality of a foreign State, so that the judgment owed to MOD in the Cubic Defense arbitration would have to qualify as property used for commercial activity in order for the FSIA exception to sovereign immunity to apply. [174] The court did not regard the judgment as commercial property; however, the court found that it was a "blocked asset" within the meaning of TRIA § 201 because it represented an interest in military equipment that Iran had acquired prior to 1981, [175] and permitted the judgment holder to attach the entire sum. One judge dissented, arguing that the judgment should be considered "at issue" before the IranU.S. Claims Tribunal in a case involving Iran's claims against the United States for non-delivery of military equipment. Although the judgment itself is not at issue, Judge Fisher reasoned, it could be used by the United States as an offset in the event Iran is eventually awarded compensation. If the judgment were considered to be at issue before the Iran-U.S. Claims Tribunal, the plaintiff would have relinquished his right to attach it in satisfaction of his judgment against Iran by accepting partial payment of compensatory damages from the U.S. Treasury pursuant to TRIA § 201.

Iran again petitioned for certiorari, which the Supreme Court granted, [176] to review whether the arbitral award is a "blocked asset" within the meaning of TRIA § 201 and whether it is "at issue" before the Iran-U.S. Claims Tribunal and thus off- limits to Elahi. The Solicitor General had filed a brief supporting certiorari on the first issue but advising against a review of the second on the basis that a determination in Iran's favor would merely mean that the award would be used to satisfy a judgment against Iran where the plaintiff had not relinquished his right to attach such assets. [177]

109TH CONGRESS: PROPOSED LEGISLATION

In addition to the bills addressing the Acree decision, (H.R. 1321 and H.Con.Res. 93, discussed supra) and one bill to provide compensation in the Roeder case (H.R. 3358), two other bills in the 109th Congress were introduced in an effort to untangle the state of litigation against terrorist States. H.R. 865/S. 1257, 109th Congress, would have repealed the Flatow Amendment and enacted a new subsection (h) after the current 28 U.S.C. § 1605 to provide an explicit cause of action against foreign terrorist States as well as their agents, officials and employees, making them liable "for personal injury or death caused by acts of that foreign State, or by that official, employee, or agent while acting within the scope of his or her office, employment, or agency, for which the courts of the United States may maintain jurisdiction under subsection (a)(7) for money damages." The bill would have authorized money damages for such actions to include economic damages, solatium, damages for pain and suffering, and punitive damages, and it would have made a foreign State vicariously liable for the actions of its officials, employees, or agents. It also contained provisions to facilitate the attachment of property in aid of execution of such judgments. The bill would have provided that the removal of a foreign State from the list of designated foreign State sponsors of terrorism would not terminate a cause of action that arose during the period of such designation, and would have made the above amendments effective retroactively to permit some plaintiffs to revive dismissed cases.

H.R. 6305/S. 3878 (109th Congress) would have directed the President to set up a claims commission to hear claims on behalf of U.S. nationals who were victims of hostage-taking by a foreign State or other terrorist party, permitting awards of up to $500,000, adjusted to reflect the annual percentage change in the Consumer Price Index. The Iran hostages and family members who were named in the Roeder case would have been eligible for additional compensation. Plaintiffs with unsatisfied judgments against terrorist States would have been permitted to bring a claim for compensation; however, recipients of compensation would have been unable to commence or maintain a lawsuit against a foreign State or its agencies and instrumentalities based on the same conduct. Members of the Armed Services taken hostage after August 2, 1990, would not have been eligible to seek compensation under the plan. Payment of awards was to come from the Hostage Victims' Fund, into which the President would have been authorized to allocate blocked assets, any funds recovered by the United States against persons for improper activity in connection with the Oil for Food Program of the United Nations, and any amounts forfeited or paid in fines for violations of various laws and regulations.

110TH CONGRESS

The National Defense Authorization Act for FY2008, § 1083

The Justice for Victims of State Sponsored Terrorism Act, S. 1944, was passed by the Senate as Section 1087 of the National Defense Authorization Act for Fiscal Year 2008 (NDAA FY2008), H.R. 1585. A modified version of the provision, a measure to facilitate lawsuits against terrorist States, was included by House and Senate Conferees as section 1083, Terrorism Exception to Immunity. [178] After President Bush vetoed H.R. 1585 due to the negative impact the measure was predicted to have on Iraq's economy and reconstruction efforts, [179] Congress passed a new version, H.R. 4986, which includes authority for the President to waive the FSIA provision with respect to Iraq. The President signed the bill into law on January 28, 2008. (P.L. 110-181).

Cause of Action and Abrogation of Immunity. Section 1083 creates a new section 1605A in title 28, U.S. Code, to incorporate the terrorist State exception to sovereign immunity under the FSIA previously codified at 28 U.S.C. § 1605(a)(7) and a cause of action against designated State sponsors of terrorism, in lieu of the Flatow Amendment. The exception to immunity and new cause of action against such States apply to cases in which money damages are sought for personal injury or death caused by certain defined terrorist acts or the provision of material support when conducted by an official, agent, or employee of the State acting within the scope of his or her office, employment, or agency, regardless of whether a U.S. official could be held liable under similar circumstances.

The cause of action is stated in subsection (c) of new § 1 605A, and covers foreign terrorist States as well as their agents, officials and employees, making them liable for personal injury or death caused by acts for which the courts of the United States may maintain jurisdiction under the subsection. It spells out the types of damages that may be recovered, including economic damages, solatium, pain and suffering, and punitive damages. [180] The foreign State is to be held vicariously liable for the actions of its officials, employees, or agents. Subsection (d) provides that, in connection with the personal injury claims it authorizes, actions may also be brought for reasonably foreseeable property loss, regardless of insurance coverage, for third party liability, and for life and property insurance policy losses.

New 28 U.S.C. § 1605A expands jurisdiction beyond cases involving U.S. nationals as a victim or claimant, expressly to include U.S. nationals, members of the Armed Forces, [181] and government employees and contractors "acting within the scope of their employment when the act upon which the claim is based occurred." As was previously the case, if the act giving rise to the suit occurred in the foreign State being sued, the claimant must first afford that State a reasonable opportunity to arbitrate the claim. The language also directs that claims be heard in cases in which the "act [of terrorism]...is related to Case Number 1 :00CV03110 (EGS) in the United States District Court for the District of Columbia," notwithstanding the other jurisdictional requirements listed. This appears intended to enable those held hostage at the U.S. embassy in Iran to bring suit, although the named case was ultimately dismissed. [182] However, the language does not expressly abrogate the Algiers Accords, making a victory for those plaintiffs seemingly unlikely in the event they refile their claims. [183]

Limitations and Procedures. The statute of limitations for claims under the act requires the commencement of an action within 10 years after April 24, 1996 or 10 years from the date on which the cause of action arose. [184] But new lawsuits are barred six months after a defendant State has been removed from the list of State sponsors of terrorism. [185]

Subsection (c)(2) amends the Victims of Crime Act by changing the effective date to October 23, 1988 (instead of December 21, 1988), and expressly includes investigations in civil matters. This will make available funds under the Victims of Crime Act, 42 U.S.C. § 10603(c), to pay costs associated with appointment of a special master to determine civil damages for the bombing of the Marine barracks in Lebanon in 1983. [186] Subsection (e) provides for the appointment of special masters to assist the court in determining claims and damages, to be funded from the Victims of Crime Act of 1984 for victims of international terrorism (42 U.S.C. § 10603c). Subsection (f) makes interlocutory appeals subject to 28 U.S.C. § 1292(b), which limits interlocutory appeals.

Lis Pendens. Section 1083 does not expressly provide for prejudgment attachment of property in anticipation of a judgment. [187] However, new 28 U.S.C. § 1605A(g) provides for the establishment of an automatic lien of lis pendens with respect to all real or tangible personal property [188] located within the judicial district that is subject to attachment in aid of execution under 28 U.S.C. § 1610 and is titled in the name of a defendant State sponsor of terrorism or any entities listed by the plaintiff as "controlled by" that State, [189] upon the filing of a notice of action in complaints that rely on the terrorism exception to the FSIA. The liens of lis pendens are expressly made enforceable pursuant to chapter 111 of title 28, U.S. Code. That chapter, however, does not establish federal procedures for enforcing lis pendens, although it does provide procedures for the enforcement of other liens in the event a defendant fails to enter an appearance. [190] Federal law provides for the application of state law regarding lis pendens, [191] and these rules vary by state. [192] Ordinarily, the doctrine of lis pendens applies only to specific property at issue in a dispute, which must be described with sufficient specificity and in some cases recorded to enable a prospective purchaser to identify it. Lis pendens applies with respect to only the property described in the notice, and cannot affect other property of a defendant. [193] It is not ordinarily available in suits seeking money judgments over matters unrelated to the property unless and until a valid judgment has been awarded. [194] It does not generally apply to negotiable instruments. [195]

Ordinarily, the purpose of filing a lien of lis pendens in civil litigation is to put third parties on notice that the property is the subject of litigation, which effectively prevents the alienation of such property, although it is not technically a lien or a prejudgment attachment. It does not prevent or invalidate transactions involving the property, and its intent is not to aid either side in the underlying dispute. [196] Its effect is to bind a person who acquires an interest in property subject to litigation to the result of the litigation as if he or she were a party to it from the outset. [197] Because the resulting cloud on title can have a detrimental effect on the value of property and the right of enjoyment, courts in some jurisdictions have the discretion to require the lis pendens proponent to post a bond when the defendant property owner can show that damages are likely in the event the notice of lis pendens is unjustified. [198] Some states require that the court expunge a lis pendens notice on evidence that the litigation is not the type contemplated by the relevant statute or that the proper procedures were followed. [199] Some state statutes permit the court to cancel a notice of lis pendens if the defendant posts bond or provides some other substitute security, if adequate relief for the claimant may be secured by these means. [200]

For recording the lis pendens liens in suits filed under section 1 605A, the clerk of the district court is required to file the notice of action "indexed by listing as defendants and all entities listed as controlled by any defendant." This appears to be intended to relieve plaintiffs of the burden of identifying specific property in the notices, but it is unclear what further measures might be required to ensure adequate notice is afforded to prospective purchasers or how it is to be determined without further process that the property is in fact subject to attachment, if the statute is interpreted to require such a showing. [201] With respect to real property, federal law ordinarily requires compliance with recordation or indexing procedures applicable in the state where the property is located in order to give constructive notice of an action pending in a United States district court. [202] State procedures typically require that notices of lis pendens affecting real estate are recorded with the local registry of deeds, although in some cases notice is deemed valid as long as the pleadings adequately describe the property at issue. [203] A notice of lis pendens that is not properly recorded may be held ineffective as to the rights of a subsequent purchaser. [204] If the filing requirement in section 1 605A(g) is deemed to replace state statutes and to give constructive notice to prospective purchasers, such purchasers who have no actual notice of the lis pendens could raise due process claims. [205]

The provision appears to have no effect on actions in state courts, which are less frequently the venue for lawsuits under the terrorism exception to the FSIA, [206] although lis pendens will be available under the applicable state law under the ordinary state court procedures for property that qualifies.

In the case of State sponsors of terror, whose property for the most part is already subject to substantial limitations on transactions, the primary utility may be the establishment of a line of priority among lien-holders, to determine which successful plaintiffs have priority in collecting from the defendant's assets. One function of a lis pendens notice is to preserve for the plaintiff a priority over all subsequent lienors, purchasers, and encumbrancers. Because the notice "relates back" to the date of its filing, other plaintiffs who seek to attach property to execute on a judgment may take such property subject to the lis pendens of plaintiffs with pending cases against the same defendant who filed notice previously, even though the complaints may have been filed at a later date and no award has yet been issued.

On the other hand, the extension of lis pendens over property owned by entities believed by plaintiffs to be "controlled by" the defendant State could potentially affect property that is not already subject to sanctions. Depending on how broadly the provision is construed, its exercise could deter transactions. In the case of States that are no longer subject to terrorism sanctions, the lis pendens provision could threaten lawful transactions and impose a new barrier to trade. [207] As long as there are pending claims or outstanding judgments against such a State under the terrorism exception to the FSIA, U.S. companies doing business with it may be subject to litigation by plaintiffs and judgment creditors who believe the U.S. company is in possession of foreign property that is subject to execution on a terrorism judgment. Any real property or tangible property in which the defendant State has an interest may be rendered effectively inalienable by lis pendens notices. If a U.S. company is selling tangible goods to a former State sponsor of terrorism, an automatic lien of lis pendens on goods purchased but not yet delivered would probably not affect the company's ability to make delivery. Companies that buy property from such a country, however, could potentially lose title of the property to plaintiffs who are awarded a judgment.

Property Subject to Execution. Subsection (b)(3) of section 1083, P.L.1 10-181 amends 28 U.S.C. § 1610 to address which property of foreign States is subject to levy in execution of terrorism judgments against those States. [208] It adds a new subsection (g) to 28 U.S.C. § 1610 to provide that the property of a foreign State against which a judgment has been entered under section 1605A, or of an agency or instrumentality of such a foreign State, "including property that is a separate juridical entity or is an interest held directly or indirectly in a separate juridical entity," is subject to attachment in aid of execution and execution upon that judgment, regardless of how much economic control over that property the foreign government actually exercises and whether the government derives profits or benefits from it. It also allows execution on the property where "establishing the property as a separate entity would entitle the foreign State to benefits in [U.S.] courts while avoiding its obligation." [209] It does not provide the President any waiver authority (except with respect to Iraq). It does not abrogate sovereign immunity of other States that have possession of any assets of a defendant State. [210]

According to the Committee report accompanying the NDAA, the purpose of the provision is to enable any property in which the foreign state has a beneficial ownership to be subject to execution for terrorism judgments, except for diplomatic and consular property. [211] The proposed language suggests that the "property" at issue is or belongs to a commercial entity in which the foreign government has an interest. The language renders subject to execution any property (including interests held directly or indirectly in a separate juridical entity) of the defendant foreign State regardless of five criteria set forth in subsection (g)(1):

(A) the level of economic control over the property by the government of the foreign state;
(B) whether the profits of the property go to that government;
(C) the degree to which officials of that government manage the property or otherwise have a hand in its daily affairs;
(D) whether that government is the sole beneficiary in interest of the property; or
(E) whether establishing the property interest as a separate entity would entitle the foreign state to benefits in [U.S.] courts while avoiding its obligations.

Courts ordinarily consider these criteria in determining whether an entity is an "alter ego" of a foreign government for liability purposes [212] or is an "agency or instrumentality" of the foreign government for purposes of determining whether it is entitled to immunity. [213] An entity that is not an agency or instrumentality of a foreign government is not entitled to sovereign immunity, but neither are its assets subject to attachment in execution of a judgment awarded against that foreign government. This is not due to sovereign immunity, but because a judgment creditor may not levy against a third party's property in order to satisfy a money judgment against a judgment debtor. [214] The new language could be read as an effort to make any entity in which the judgment debtor foreign State (including its separate agencies and instrumentalities) has any interest liable for the terrorism-related judgments awarded against that State, [215] even if the entity is not itself an agency or instrumentality of the State. [216] The conferee's intent to enable execution on property in which the defendant state has beneficial ownership [217] seems contradicted by the statement that the property is subject to execution regardless of whether the "profits of the property go to that government" or "whether that government is the sole beneficiary in interest of the property."

On the other hand, subparagraph (3) addresses the rights of third parties who also have an interest in the property that may be subject to levy in execution on a judgment. Captioned "Third-Party Joint Property Holders," it states that nothing in the new section 1610(g) is to be construed as superceding the authority of a court to prevent the impairment of an interest held by a person "who is not liable in the action giving rise to a judgment." The conference report states the intent of the conferees was to "encourage the courts to protect the property interests of such innocent third parties by using their inherent authority, on a case-by-case basis, under the applicable procedures governing execution on judgment and attachment in anticipation of judgment." [218] Nonetheless, this savings language is not easily squared with the provision's stated applicability to indirectly held property, without regard to the benefit the debtor government derives from the property. Moreover, agencies or instrumentalities of foreign governments have not generally been considered to be liable for the debts of the foreign government itself or for other agencies or instrumentalities. Subparagraph (3) could be read to permit the court to protect their assets as well, although subparagraph (1) appears intended to make their assets available to satisfy terrorism judgments against the foreign State. [219]

Blocked and Regulated Property under Sanctions Regulations. New subsection (g)(2), captioned "U.S. sovereign immunity inapplicable," would make a property described in (g)(1) that is regulated by reason of U.S. sanctions not immune by reason of such regulation from execution to satisfy a judgment. It would not explicitly waive U.S. sovereign immunity, [220] but appears designed to defeat provisions in the sanctions regulations that make blocked property effectively immune from court action. [221] In this respect, it echoes language in current § 1610(f)(1), except that it applies only to regulated property rather than property that is blocked or regulated pursuant to sanctions regimes, and it would not be subject to the presidential waiver in § 1620(f)(3). Unlike § 201 of TRIA (28 U.S.C. § 1610 note), the new language applies to regulated rather than blocked assets, [222] and it allows assets to be attached in aid of enforcing punitive damages.

Despite its caption, new section (g)(2) will not likely make funds in the U.S. Treasury, such as any funds set aside to pay a debt to Iran [223] or those held in the Foreign Military Sales (FMS) trust fund account presently under dispute between Iran and the United States, reachable by judgment creditors. [224] Even if the provision is read to waive U.S. sovereign immunity, these funds remain the property of the United States and could not be used to satisfy the debt of another party. A contrary interpretation of the provision might implicate other policy concerns. To allow attachment of the FMS trust fund would eliminate the U.S.' ability to claim a right to those funds in subrogation of payments made pursuant to VTVPA § 2002 in the event the Iran-U.S. Claims Tribunal issues an award in Iran's favor, and could also breach U.S. obligations under the Algiers Accords. New subsection (g)(2) will not likely affect the rights of those who received U.S. funds in partial payment of their judgments against Iran, who will likely remain barred by the applicable provisions of VTVPA § 2002 from attaching certain property or attempting (in certain cases) to collect the punitive portions of their damages.

Application to Pending Cases. Subsection (c) of the § 1083 spells out how its amendments are to apply to pending cases. It states that the amendments apply to any claim arising under them as well as to any action brought under current 28 U.S.C. § 1605(a)(7) or the Flatow Amendment that "relied on either of these provisions as creating a cause of action" and that "has been adversely affected on the grounds that either or both of these provisions fail to create a cause of action against the state," and that "is still before the courts in any form, including appeal or motion under rule 60(b) of the Federal Rules of Civil Procedure...."[225] In cases brought under the older provisions, the federal district court in which the case originated is required, on motion by the plaintiffs within 60 days after enactment, to treat the case as if it had been brought under the new provisions, apparently to include reinstating vacated judgments. The subsection also states that the "defenses of res judicata, collateral estoppel and limitation period are waived" in any reinstated judgment or refiled action. The language does not indicate how pending cases in state courts are to be handled. The provision does not appear to permit the refiling of actions to override decisions construing the statute of limitations strictly. However, it might be read to permit post-judgment relief to pursue increased awards, possibly including punitive damages, where the application of state law or other law [226] to a claim resulted in a lower award than would have been permitted pursuant to the Flatow. Amendment if it had been read to provide a federal cause of action. [227] It could be interpreted to permit the amendment of judgments against officials in their private capacity to make the foreign State responsible for the debt.

In addition, subparagraph (3) permits the filing of new cases involving incidents that are already the subject of a timely-filed action under any of the terrorism exceptions to the FSIA. This appears to allow victims of State-supported terrorism to bring suit notwithstanding the limitation time for filing, so long as another victim of the same terrorist act had brought suit in time. It may allow claimants previously not covered by the exceptions, such as foreign nationals working for the United States government overseas who were injured in a terrorist attack, to bring a lawsuit despite expiration of the statute of limitations. It may also allow plaintiffs with previous judgments to pursue new judgments based on the same terrorist incident but citing the new cause of action. [228] Such actions must be filed within sixty days after enactment or the date of entry of judgment in the original action. [229] Refiled actions and actions related to previous claims are to be permitted to go forth even if the foreign State is no longer designated as a State sponsor of terrorism, as long as the original action was filed when the State was on the list of terrorist States. (28 U.S.C. § 1605A(a)(2)(A)(i)(II)).

Although subsection (c) refers to "pending cases," it appears to encompass finally adjudicated cases in which litigants have, as of the date of enactment (January 28, 2008), filed a motion for relief from final judgment under Rule 60(b) or any other motion that might be available to allow discretionary relief after a final judgment is rendered and appeals are no longer possible. Ordinarily, a change in statutory law may be applied to civil cases that arose prior to its enactment, if Congress makes clear its intent in this regard, [230] but only in cases still pending before the courts and those filed after enactment. To the extent that § 1083 is read to require courts to reopen final judgments and previously dismissed cases, or reinstate vacated judgments, the provision may be vulnerable to invalidation as an improper exercise of judicial powers by Congress. [231] A similar objection may be raised with respect to the waiver of legal defenses — while it is well-established that Congress can waive legal defenses in actions against the United States, [232] an effort to abrogate valid legal defenses of other parties could raise constitutional due process and separation of powers issues.

Subsection (c)(4) of section 1083 states that section 1503 of the Emergency Wartime Supplemental Appropriations Act (EWSAA) (PL 108-11) "has [n]ever authorized, directly or indirectly, the making inapplicable of any provision of chapter 97 of title 28, United States Code, or the removal of the jurisdiction of any court of the United States." This provision would appear to be aimed at ensuring that no court construes section 1503 of EWSAA to restore Iraq's sovereign immunity with respect to actions involving terrorist acts that occurred while Iraq was designated a State sponsor of terrorism, as the government has continued to argue despite the D.C. Circuit's ruling in the Acree case that EWSAA did not affect the FSIA. [233] However, the presidential waiver authority in subsection (d) appears to obviate the effect of the language. [234]

The Consolidated Appropriations Act, P.L. 110-161 (Libya)

The Consolidated Appropriations Act for FY2008 (H.R. 2764), § 654 prohibits the expenditure of any funds made available in that act to finance directly any assistance for Libya unless "the Secretary of State certifies to the Committees on Appropriations that the Government of Libya has made the final settlement payments to the Pan Am 103 victims' families, paid to the La Belle Disco bombing victims the agreed upon settlement amounts, and is engaging in good faith settlement discussions regarding other relevant terrorism cases." The Secretary is further required to submit a report within 180 days of enactment describing State Department efforts to facilitate a resolution of these cases and U.S. commercial activities in Libya's energy sector. [235]

Proposals to Waive § 1083 for Former State Sponsors of Terrorism

Although new lawsuits are barred six months after a defendant State has been removed from the list of State sponsors of terrorism, [236] new cases based on a terrorist act that is or was already the subject of a lawsuit under the terrorism exception to the FSIA are permitted within 60 days of enactment of the NDAA (signed into law January 28, 2008) or 60 days within the date of entry of judgment in the "original lawsuit." [237] Accordingly, without intervention by Congress, a State would remain subject to new lawsuits based on certain acts of terrorism that occurred while it was designated a state sponsor of terrorism until 60 days after the entry of final judgment in cases currently pending. The threat of new lawsuits or attachment of property in satisfaction of prior judgments could impede the resumption of ordinary trade with that State.

Although new 28 U.S.C. § 1610(g) may not permit the attachment of property belonging to U.S. companies doing business with a former State sponsor of terrorism subject to section 1083 (at least so long as that government has no interest of its own in the property), the measure could make commercial transactions more difficult. Judgment holders would likely seek to attach goods purchased by the debtor government as well as financial instruments used to pay for goods or services or to secure contract performance. If judgment holders succeed in seizing property or debts in the possession of a U.S. company, the contracting government could seek to hold the company liable for breach of contract for failing to make payment or delivery, as the case may be. Or the government could seek to justify its own breach or early termination of a contract, which could also result in losses to the U.S. company involved. Although it seems likely that a U.S. court would not find the U.S. company in breach of contract for having submitted to a judicial order, the contract in question may call for disputes to be resolved according to foreign law or in a foreign forum or through international arbitration, in which case the outcome may be less certain. The risk of litigation, which is unlikely to be without cost even if successful, may serve as a deterrent to trade. [238] If a former State sponsor of terrorism chooses not to open accounts or establish standby letters of credit in financial institutions subject to U.S. jurisdiction, trade between U.S. companies and that country could become more difficult and riskier for the U.S. companies involved, and the foreign State may avoid risk by choosing business partners outside the United States.

Exemption for Libya (S. 3370). U.S. businesses seeking to establish a commercial relationship with Libya expressed concern that § 1083 will harm U.S.- Libya trade. [239] The Bush Administration, which has touted renewed U.S. investment in Libya and growth in bilateral trade as beneficial to the U.S. economy and as important tools for reestablishing relations with a reformed state sponsor of terrorism, appears to share their view. [240] Nearly $1.7 billion has been awarded against Libya, with an additional $5.3 billion awarded against certain named Libyan officials, [241] and with some 20 additional cases pending. The State Department announced that settlement negotiations to resolve outstanding cases against Libya were ongoing, [242] and asked Congress to amend section 1083 to permit waivers in the case of all States that are removed from the list of designated State sponsors of terrorism. Senator Biden introduced a separate bill negotiated by the Administration, S. 3370, to exempt Libya from terror-related lawsuits if it agrees to compensate certain U.S. victims under a claims settlement agreement with the United States. [243]

S. 3370, the "Libyan Claims Resolution Act," was enacted on August 4, 2008. It provides an exception to the FSIA for Libya in the event Libya signs an international agreement ("claims agreement") with the United States to settle terrorism-related claims and to provide fair compensation. It contains a sense of the Congress in support of the President's efforts "to provide fair compensation to all nationals of the United States who have terrorism-related claims against Libya." The statute authorizes the Secretary of State to designate one or more "entities" within the United States to assist in the provision of compensation. It does not indicate whether the designated entity is to have a role in adjudicating claims, or whether the amount of compensation and identity of claimants eligible for compensation are to be specifically set forth in the claims agreement. It appears that the government is to receive funds pursuant to an agreement with Libya, which it would then turn over to the designated entity for dispersal to claimants, although there is no express requirement to this effect in the statute. All of the entity's property that is related to the claims agreement would then be immune from judicial attachment, and the entity itself would be immune from lawsuits related to actions it takes to implement a claims agreement. A designated entity will not be subject to the Government Corporation Control Act. [244]

If the Secretary of State certifies to Congress that sufficient funds have been received under the claims agreement, the statute will provide immunity to Libya, including its agencies and instrumentalities as well as its officials, employees, and agents, for all claims brought under the terrorism exception to the FSIA, either under the previous version of the statute or as amended by § 1083 of the FY08 NDAA, whether the suits are brought in federal or state courts. The statute provides immunity to property belonging to Libya, including its agencies and instrumentalities, and the property of Libyan agents, officials, and employees, from attachment in aid of execution or similar judicial process under the FSIA terrorism exception. In order for the funds received by the government to be sufficient for the purposes of the certification under the bill, they must be sufficient to cover settlements Libya has agreed to pay to victims of the Pan Am 103 airliner bombing and the La Belle Disco bombing, as well as to provide "fair compensation" to U.S. nationals who have pending cases against Libya for wrongful death or physical injury arising under section 28 U.S.C. § 1605A (including previous actions that have been given effect as if they had been filed under § 1605A). It appears that the amount of fair compensation is left to the discretion of the Secretary of State. It is unclear how the entity designated to assist in the dispersal of the funds is to determine how much to provide to each of the claimants. There is no express requirement that the designated entity disperse the funds.

The provision does not explicitly state that only claims described in the certification requirement would be compensated, but this seems to be a fair inference. Under this interpretation, no compensation is envisioned in the case of claimants who are not beneficiaries of a settlement agreement in the Pan Am 103 and La Belle Disco cases unless they have a pending case under § 1605A for wrongful death or physical injury. [245] Claims that would otherwise be permitted under § 1605A, for example, a claim for solatium or intentional infliction of emotional distress related to the hostage-taking of a family member, would not likely be compensated under the bill. It appears that finally adjudicated cases are not covered, in which case unsatisfied judgments against Libya and its officials will likely be unenforceable. [246] Claimants do not appear to have any recourse in court to dispute the amount or a denial of compensation under the proposal, although a claim against the United States for an uncompensated "taking" in violation of the Fifth Amendment would not be foreclosed.

Other Bills in the 110th Congress

H.R. 3346 is substantially identical to H.R. 6305 as introduced in the 109th Congress, except that it makes a provision for returning assets from the Hostage Victims' Fund to a foreign State after its status as a terrorist State has been terminated, provided all claims have been paid or the President determines that sufficient funds remain available to pay remaining claims. It is unclear whether these requirements refer to claims against the foreign State whose terrorist designation has been lifted, or whether claims against all terrorist States must be satisfied prior to the return of any frozen assets. H.R. 3369 contains the same provisions as H.R. 3346, but also specifically includes plaintiffs in Hegna v. Islamic Republic of Iran [247] among the class of persons who would be eligible to seek compensation from the Hostage Victims' Fund. The bill also expands the provision regarding additional compensation for former hostages held at the U.S. embassy in Iran to cover any person who was kidnaped by Hezbollah on December 4, 1984, and transferred to Iran. This language appears intended to cover Charles Hegna, except that it is unclear whether he is also a "person who qualifies for payment under subsection a(3)," depending on whether his estate is deemed to be a "person." Children and spouses of the specified victims at the time of the hostage-taking would be eligible to receive 50 percent of the "total amount of compensation paid to the person taken hostage." This subparagraph could exclude the Hegna plaintiffs as well, since Charles Hegna was murdered by the hijackers and never received compensation, unless it is read to encompass all compensation his family might recover under subsection a(1) or otherwise in satisfaction of their judgment. It is unclear whether the compensation received by the family members under section 2002 of the Victims of Trafficking Act would also be included in the "total amount of compensation." H.R. 394 would abrogate the Algiers Accords, to the extent it prevents former hostages from maintaining lawsuits against Iran, and establish a fund to pay the former hostages their families compensation derived from liquidated frozen assets and the Iranian FMS account.

S. 1839, passed by the Senate with unanimous consent on October 18, 2007, would require the Administration to submit to Congress a report every six months detailing the status of outstanding legal claims by American victims against the government of Libya for acts described in section 1605(a)(7) of title 28, United States Code. (Libya was removed from the list of State Sponsors of Terrorism on May 15, 2006 [248]). The reports would continue until the Secretary of State certifies there are no such claims left unresolved, and would be required to include the Administration's own efforts on behalf of those victims and the status of their negotiations with Libya to obtain payment.

H.R. 5167, the Justice for Victims of Torture and Terrorism Act, would repeal the waiver provision for Iraq passed in P.L. 110-181 (§ 1083(d)) and nullify any existing waivers issued pursuant to that provision.

SUITS AGAINST THE UNITED STATES FOR "TERRORIST" ACTS

At least two of the States affected by the FSIA exception appear to have enacted legislation allowing their citizens to file suit against the United States for violations of human rights or interference in the countries' internal affairs. Cuba reportedly allows such suits for violations of human rights; and at least two judgments assessing billions of dollars in damages against the U.S. have apparently been handed down. [249]

Iran reportedly has authorized suits against foreign States for intervention in the internal affairs of the country and for terrorist activities resulting in the death, injury, or financial loss of Iranian nationals; and at least one judgment for half a billion dollars in damages has been handed down against the United States. [250] The judgment was awarded to a businessman who brought suit against the United States for "kidnapping, false imprisonment, using force, battering, abusing and ultimately inflicting physical and psychological injuries" in connection with his arrest by undercover U.S. Customs agents in the Bahamas for violating U.S. sanctions regulations. [251] The judgment creditor in the case reportedly sought to attach the defunct U.S. embassy in Tehran to satisfy the judgment. [252]

Conclusion

The 1996 amendments to the FSIA allowing victims of terrorism to sue designated foreign States for damages in U.S. courts were enacted with broad political support in Congress. But subsequent difficulties in obtaining payment of the substantial damages assessed for the most part in default judgments by the courts, and subsequent efforts in Congress to facilitate or allow such payment out of the defendant States' frozen assets in the United States, have raised issues fraught with both emotion and complexity. Matters of effectiveness, fairness, diplomacy, and possible reciprocal action against U.S. assets abroad have all entered the debate. In addition, the issue has pitted the compensation of victims of terrorism against U.S. foreign policy goals, including compliance with specific international obligations and the decision to use funds for the reconstruction of Iraq.

U.S. courts have awarded victims of terrorism more than $19 billion in judgments against State sponsors of terrorism and their officials under the terrorism exception to the FSIA. Some claimants were able to collect portions of their judgments under § 2002 of the Victims of Trafficking Act, while those not covered have been left largely to compete with each other to lay claim to the blocked assets of terrorist States for satisfaction of the compensatory damages portions of their judgments. In the case of Iran — the defendant in the largest number of suits filed, those blocked assets are virtually non-existent; and Presidential Determination 2003- 23 made Iraq's blocked assets unavailable to pay subsequently awarded judgments against Iraq. Most of the Cuban assets made available by § 2002 to satisfy judgments have also been liquidated to pay to judgment creditors. [253]

An appellate court decision in 2004 holding that no cause of action exists under the FSIA to sue terrorist States themselves, as opposed to their employees, officials, and agents, led courts to apply domestic state tort law to lawsuits against terrorist States based on the domicile of the victim, resulting in some disparity of relief available to victims. Confusion about the definition of an "agency or instrumentality" of a foreign State also brought uncertainty to these lawsuits. The Supreme Court in the Elahi case clarified the importance of distinguishing between "agencies and instrumentalities" and foreign States themselves, but did not address any of the other issues raised by the terrorism exception to the FSIA.

Section 1083 of the FY2008 National Defense Appropriations Act will likely clarify the existence of a federal cause of action against State sponsors of terrorism, but U.S. nationals with outstanding causes of action against Iraq may call on Congress for some form of redress. The total amount of judgments against

State sponsors of terrorism and former State sponsors of terrorism is likely to increase more rapidly, especially if § 1803(c) is deemed valid to permit the refiling of cases, the reinstatement of vacated judgments, or the upward amendment of final awards, as well as the filing of new cases for which the statute of limitations has already expired. Whether more assets of those States will become available to satisfy those judgments is less certain. Making the assets of separate agencies and instrumentalities available to satisfy judgments may increase the total assets available for levy in the short term, but may also lead such entities to avoid future transactions that would put their assets at risk. An increase in transactions with debtor States is likely to occur only with respect to those States that are no longer subject to antiterrorism sanctions, in which case the use of any assets that come into the jurisdiction of the United States to satisfy judgments may act as a barrier to trade notwithstanding the lifting of sanctions. On the other hand, if the terrorism exception to the FSIA results in a decrease in terrorist attacks affecting the interests of U.S. persons, such judgments should become less common with the passage of time and the statute of limitations.

APPENDIX A. JUDGMENTS AGAINST TERRORIST STATES

Table A-1. Judgments Against Terrorist States Covered by VTVPA § 2002 (P.L. 106-386)

Judgment	Compensatory Damages Awarded	Punitive Damages Awarded	Amount Paid Pursuant to § 2002 (Including Interest)	Procedure Used
Alejandre v. Republic of Cuba, 996 F.Supp. 1239 (S.D. Fla. 1997).	$50 million	$137.7 million	$96,708,652.03	Paid from liquidated Cuban assets
Flatow v. Islamic Republic of Iran, 999 F. Supp. 2d 1 (D.D.C. 1998).	$22.5 million	$225 million	$26,002,690.15	100% option (appropriated funds)
Cicippio v. Islamic Republic of Iran, 18 F. Supp. 2d 62 (D.D.C. 1998).	$65 million	$0	$73,260,501.72	100% option (appropriated funds)
Anderson v. Islamic Republic of Iran, 90 F. Supp. 2d 107 (D.D.C. 2000).	$41.2 million	$300 million	$47,315,791.80	110% option (appropriated funds)
Eisenfeld v. Islamic Republic of Iran, 172 F. Supp. 2d 1 (D.D.C. 2000).	$24.7 million	$300 million	$27,365,288.83	100% option (appropriated funds)
Higgins v. Islamic Republic of Iran, 2000 WL 33674311 (D.D.C. 2000).	$55.4 million	$300 million	$57,086,233.16	100% option (appropriated funds)

Judgment	Compensatory Damages Awarded	Punitive Damages Awarded	Amount Paid Pursuant to § 2002 (Including Interest)	Procedure Used
Sutherland v. Islamic Republic of Iran, 151 F. Supp. 2d 27 (D.D.C. 2001).	$53.4 million	$300 million	$56,084,467.27	One claimant chose the 110% option, the others the 100% option (appropriated funds)
Polhill v. Islamic Republic of Iran, 2001 WL 34157508 (D.D.C. 2001).	$31.5 million	$300 million	$35,041,877.36	110% option (appropriated funds)
Jenco v. Islamic Republic of Iran, 154 F. Supp. 2d 27 (D.D.C. 2001).	$14.64 million	$300 million	$14,865,685.76	100% option (appropriated funds)
Wagner v. Islamic Republic of Iran, 172 F. Supp. 2d 128 (D.D.C. 2001).	$16.28 million	$300 million	$18,032,569.00	110% option (appropriated funds)
Stethem v. Islamic Republic of Iran, 201 F. Supp. 2d 78 (D.D.C. 2002).	$21.2 million	$300 million (jointly with Carlson)	$21,579,737.64	100% option (appropriated funds)
Carlson v. Islamic Republic of Iran, 201 F. Supp. 2d 78 (D.D.C. 2002).	$7.8 million	$300 million (jointly with Stethem)	$8,784,584.90	110% option (appropriated funds)
Martinez v. Republic of Cuba, No. 13-1999-CA 018208 (Miami-Dade Co., Fla., Cir. Ct. 2001).	$7.1 million	$20 million	at least $7.1 million[1]	Paid from Cuban assets

Judgment	Compensatory Damages Awarded	Punitive Damages Awarded	Amount Paid Pursuant to § 2002 (Including Interest)	Procedure Used
Cases added by P.L. 107-228 and TRIA:				
Elahi v. Islamic Republic of Iran, 124 F. Supp. 2d 97 (D.D.C. 2000).	$11.7 million	$300 million	$2,342,729.89	Pro rata payment (appropriated funds)
Mousa v. Islamic Republic of Iran, 238 F. Supp. 2d 1 (D.D.C. 2001).	$12 million	$120 million	$2,394,606.04	Pro rata payment (appropriated funds)
Weinstein v. Islamic Republic of Iran, 184 F. Supp. 2d 13 (D.D.C. 2002).	$33 million	$150 million	$6,634,687.87	Pro rata payment (appropriated funds)
Hegna v. Islamic Republic of Iran, No. 1:00CV00716 (D.D.C. 2002).	$42 million	$333 million	$8,387,121.10	Pro rata payment (appropriated funds)
Kapar v. Islamic Republic of Iran, C.A. No. 02-CV-78-HHK (D.D.C. 2004).	$13.5 million	$0	approx. $2.5 million[a]	Pro rata payment (appropriated funds)

Note: Information on the amounts paid under § 2002 was provided by the Office of Foreign Assets Control (OFAC) and is current as of July 2003. Claimants in the first tier (Flatow through Carlson) choosing the 100 percent option were entitled to receive 100 percent of the compensatory damages awarded plus post-judgment interest on condition that they relinquish any further right to compensatory damages and any right to satisfy their punitive damages award out of the blocked assets of the terrorist State (including diplomatic property), debts owed by the United States to the terrorist State as the result of judgments by the Iran-U.S. Claims Tribunal, and any property that is at issue in claims against the United States before that and other international tribunals (such as Iran's Foreign Military Sales account). Claimants who chose the 110 percent option were entitled to receive 110 percent of the compensatory damages awarded plus post-judgment interest on condition they relinquish any further right to obtain compensatory and punitive damages. The claimants in the second tier (added by P.L. 107-228 and TRIA) divided the amount remaining in the fund on a pro rata basis, and were not required to give up their right to recover additional compensatory damages, except from property at issue before an international tribunal.

a. These figures have not been confirmed by OFAC, but are estimates of amounts payable under the statute.

Table A-2. Judgments Against Terrorist States Not Covered by VTVPA § 2002

Judgment	Compensatory Damages Awarded	Punitive Damages Awarded
Bakhtiar v. Islamic Republic of Iran, Civil Action No. 02-00092 (HHK) (D.D.C. 2008).	$12,000,000	$0.00
Bennett v. Islamic Republic of Iran, 507 F. Supp. 2d 117 (D.D.C. 2007).	$12,904,548.00	$0.00
Ben-Rafael v. Islamic Republic of Iran, 2008 WL 485091 (D.D.C. 2008).	$62,441,839.00	$0.00
Blais v. Islamic Republic of Iran, 459 F. Supp. 2d 40 (D.D.C. 2006).	$28,801,792.00	$0.00
Bodoff v. Islamic Republic of Iran, 424 F. Supp. 2d 74 (D.D.C. 2006).	$16,988,300.00	$300,000,000.00
Campuzano v. Islamic Republic of Iran, 281 F. Supp. 2d 258 (D.D.C. 2003).	$112,463,608.00	$300,000,000.00
Cicippio-Puleo v. Islamic Republic of Iran, Civil Action No. 01-01496 (HHK) (D.D.C. 2005).	$91,000,000.00	$0.00
Cronin v. Islamic Republic of Iran, 238 F. Supp. 2d 222 (D.D.C. 2002).	$1,200,000.00	$300,000,000.00
Daliberti v. Republic of Iraq, 146 F. Supp. 2d 19 (D.D.C. 2001).	$18,823,289.00	$0.00
Dammarell v. Islamic Republic of Iran, 2006 WL 2583043 (D.D.C 2006).	$316,919,657.00	$0.00
Dodge v. Islamic Republic of Iran, 2004 WL 5353873 (D.D.C. 2004).	$5,670,000.00	$0.00
Estate of Heiser v. Islamic Republic of Iran, 466 F. Supp. 2d 229 (D.D.C. 2006).	$254,431,903.00	$0.00
Estate of Bayani v. Islamic Republic of Iran, Civil Action No. 04-01712 (HHK), 2007 WL 4116167 (D.D.C. 2007).	$66,331,500.00	$400,000,000.00 (assessed against the Iranian Revolutionary Guard Corp)
Greenbaum v. Islamic Republic of Iran, 451 F. Supp. 2d 90 (D.D.C 2006).	$19,879,023.00	$0.00
Haim v. Islamic Republic of Iran, 425 F. Supp. 2d 56 (D.D.C 2006).	$16,000,000.00	$0.00
Hausler v. Cuba, No. 02-12475 CA04 (Miami-Dade Co., Fla., 11th Cir. Ct. decided Dec. 14, 2006)	$1,000,000.00	$3,000,000.00
Hill v. Republic of Iraq, 175 F. Supp. 2d 36 (D.D.C. 2001).	$94,110,000.00	$300,000,000.00

Judgment	Compensatory Damages Awarded	Punitive Damages Awarded
Holland v. Islamic Republic of Iran, 496 F. Supp. 2d 1 (D.D.C. 2005).	$25,241,486.00	$0.00
Jacobsen v. Islamic Republic of Iran, Civil Action No. 02-1365 (JR) (D.D.C. 2006).	$6,400,000.00	$0.00
Kerr v. Islamic Republic of Iran, 245 F. Supp. 2d 59 (D.D.C. 2003).	$33,025,296.00	$0.00
Levin v. Islamic Republic of Iran, Civil Action No. 05-02494 (GK), 2007 WL 4564399 (D.D.C. 2008).	$28,807,719.00	$0.00
McCarthy v. Republic of Cuba, No. 01-28628 CA04 (Miami-Dade Co., Fla., 11th Cir. Ct. decided Apr. 17, 2003).	$67,000,000.00	$0.00
Nikbin v. Islamic Republic of Iran, 517 F. Supp. 2d 416 (D.D.C. 2007).	$2,600,000.00	$0.00
Peterson v. Islamic Republic of Iran, 515 F. Supp. 2d 25 (D.D.C. 2007).	$2,656,944,877.00	$0.00
Prevatt v. Islamic Republic of Iran, 421 F. Supp. 2d 152 (D.D.C. 2006).	$2,500,000.00	$0.00
Price v. Libya, 384 F. Supp. 2d 120 (D.D.C. 2005).	$17,786,221.85	$0.00
Pugh v. Libya, 530 F. Supp. 2d 216 (D.D.C. 2008).	$1,635,583,302.00*	$0.00
Rafii v. Islamic Republic of Iran, Civil Action No. 01-850 (CKK) (D.D.C. 2002).	$5,000,000.00	$300,000,000.00
Regier v. Islamic Republic of Iran, 281 F. Supp. 2d 87 (D.D.C. 2003).	$5,321,520.00	$0.00
Rux v. Republic of Sudan, 495 F. Supp. 2d 541 (E.D. Va. 2007).	$7,956,344.00	$0.00
Salazar v. Islamic Republic of Iran, 370 F. Supp. 2d 105 (D.D.C. 2005).	$18,297,000.00	$0.00
Sisso v. Islamic Republic of Iran, 2007 WL 2007582 (D.D.C. 2007).	$5,000,000.00	$0.00
Smith v. Islamic Emirate of Afghanistan, 262 F. Supp. 2d 217 (S.D.N.Y. 2003).	$64,002,483.19 (damages for which Iraq is responsible)	$0.00
Steen v. Islamic Republic of Iran, 2003 WL 21672820 (D.D.C. 2003).	$42,750,000.00	$300,000,000.00
Stern v. Islamic Republic of Iran, 271 F. Supp. 2d 286 (D.D.C. 2003).	$10,000,000.00	$300,000,000.00

Judgment	Compensatory Damages Awarded	Punitive Damages Awarded
Suarez v. Republic of Cuba, No. 05-25387 CA-27 (Miami-Dade Co., Fla., 11th Cir. Ct. 2008).	$127,750,000.00	$125,000,000.00
Surette v. Islamic Republic of Iran, 231 F. Supp. 2d 260 (D.D.C. 2002).	$18,961,284.00	$300,000,000.00
Tracy v. Islamic Republic of Iran, 2003 U.S. Dist. LEXIS 15844 (D.D.C. 2003).	$18,509,000.00	$0.00
Turner v. Islamic Republic of Iran, 2002 U.S. Dist. LEXIS 26730 (D.D.C. 2002).	$27,310,000.00	$300,000,000.00
Valore v. Islamic Republic of Iran, 478 F. Supp. 2d 101 (D.D.C. 2007).	Not yet determined	$0.00
Vera v. Republic of Cuba, No. 01-31216-CA-01 (Miami-Dade Co., Fla., 11th Cir. Ct. 2008).	$44,630,000.00	$94,630,000.00
Weininger v. Republic of Cuba, No. 03-22920 CA 20 (Miami-Dade Co., Fla., 11th Cir. Ct. 2004).	$21,362,000.00	$65,000,000.00
Wear v. Islamic Republic of Iran, Civil Action No. 01-1303 (TPJ) (D.D.C. 2003).	$11,430,000.00	$300,000,000.00
Welch v. Islamic Republic of Iran, Civil Action No. A01-863(CKK)(AK) (D.D.C. 2007).	$32,698,304.00	$0.00

Note: These are cases brought under the terrorism exception to the Foreign Sovereign Immunities Act that are not entitled to compensation from the fund created by § 2002. As of the date of this report, the total value of such judgments is more than $14 billion. A total of $5,866,557,007.04 of this figure is compensatory damages; the remainder represents approximately $3.3 billion in punitive damages and $5.27 billion in damages awarded against foreign officials in their personal capacity. This figure does not include the vacated award in the Acree case or compensatory awards against Cuba and Iraq known to have been satisfied from frozen assets). For satisfied judgments against Iraq, see supra note 111. For satisfied judgments against Cuba, see Weininger v. Cuba, 462 F. Supp. 2d 457 (S.D.N.Y. 2006). Judgment creditors in this category of cases may attempt to collect compensatory (but not punitive damages) from all blocked assets of the defendant State under TRIA § 201, except for diplomatic and consular property where the President has issued a waiver, and may collect any damages (punitive as well as compensatory) from any other property of the judgment creditor State that is not entitled to immunity under 28 U.S.C. § 1610, as amended by P.L. 110-18,1 § 1083 (except for those with judgments against Iraq).

a. Plaintiffs were also awarded $5,268,100,143.00 against six named Libyan officials for their role in the bombing of a French airliner on September 19, 1989 over Niger, Africa, which killed 107 passengers and crew. The sum represents treble damages available to victims of terrorism under 18 U.S.C. § 2333. Because this portion of the judgment was awarded against the officials in their personal capacities, it is not enforceable against the Libyan government unless the judgment is permitted to be amended pursuant to § 1083 of the FY2008 NDAA. Under the Libyan Claims Resolution Act, the property of Libya and its officials are immune from attachment to enforce this judgment.

APPENDIX B. ASSETS OF TERRORIST STATES

Table B-1. Amount of Assets of Terrorist States

State	Blocked Assets in millions of dollars	Non-blocked Assets in millions of dollars	Outstanding Damages in millions of dollars
Cuba	$196.1	$0	$436.4
Iran	$1.1	$51	$9,600.3
Iraq	—	—	$364
Libya	—	—	$1,653
North Korea	$31.7	$0	$0
Sudan	$80.6	$0	$8.0
Syria	$0	$51	$0
Total	$309.5	$102	$11,398

Note: Information pertaining to blocked assets is from the Calendar Year 2006 Fifteenth Annual Report to the Congress on Assets in the United States of Terrorist Countries and International Terrorism Program Designees (September 2007), which was prepared by the Office of Foreign Assets Control (OFAC) in the Department of the Treasury. These values may fluctuate. They do not include the values of diplomatic and consular real property owned by Iran. Figures for non-blocked assets include property of individuals and entities not necessarily associated with the government of the State listed.

Outstanding damages are approximate figures compiled by CRS. They include unsatisfied portions of judgments that plaintiffs are entitled to enforce against the defendant State, not including post-judgment interest.

REFERENCE

[1] 28 U.S.C. §§ 1602 et seq. The exception allows suit to be brought against the agencies and instrumentalities of such States as well.

[2] P.L. 104-132, Title II, §221 (April 23, 1996); 110 Stat. 1241; 28 U.S.C. § 1605(a)(7).

[3] "Civil Liability for Acts of State-Sponsored Terrorism," P.L. 104-208, Title I, §101(c) [Title V, § 589] (September 30, 1996), 110 Stat. 3009-172; codified at 28 U.S.C. § 1605 note, provides: (a) an official, employee, or agent of a foreign state designated as a state sponsor of terrorism designated under section 6(j) of the Export Administration Act of 1979 (50 App. U.S.C. 2405(j)) while acting within the scope of his or her office, employment, or agency shall be liable to a United States national or the national's legal representative for personal injury or death caused by acts of that official, employee, or agent for which the courts of the United States may maintain jurisdiction under section 1605(a)(7) of title 28, United States Code, for money damages which may include economic damages, solatium, pain, and suffering, and punitive damages if the acts were among those described in section 1605(a)(7). (b) Provisions related to statute of limitations and limitations on discovery that would apply to an action brought under 28 U.S.C. 1605(f) and (g) shall also apply to actions brought under this section. No action shall be maintained under this action if an official, employee, or agent of the United States, while acting within the scope of his or her office, employment, or agency would not be liable for such acts if carried out within the United States.

[4] The FSIA provides that States are not liable for punitive damages but that such damages may be awarded against their agencies and instrumentalities. See 28 U.S.C. § 1606. Although the D.C. Circuit has found that punitive damages do not apply to agencies of foreign governments that perform primarily governmental rather than commercial services because such agencies are considered to be the State itself rather than an agent, Roeder v. Islamic Republic of Iran, 333 F.3d 228, 234 (D.C. Cir. 2003), cert. denied, 124 S.Ct. 2836 (2004), some courts continued to award punitive damages against foreign military and intelligence agencies. The Supreme Court vacated and remanded a decision that had treated the Ministry of Defense (MOD) of Iran as an "agency or instrumentality" for the purpose of determining immunity of its property to execution to satisfy a judgment, but did not explain how the court was to determine the proper characterization of an entity. Total punitive damages awarded under the terrorism exception

to the FSIA now amount to nearly $7.3 billion (excluding any vacated awards). Total compensatory damages under the exception amount to about $6.6 billion. Another $5.3 billion was awarded against six Libyan officials in their personal capacities. See Appendix A

[5] The Schooner Exchange, 11 U.S. (7 Cranch) 116, 137 (1812) (holding a French warship to be immune from the jurisdiction of a U.S. court). In Berizzi Bros. Co. v. S.S. Pesaro, 271 U.S. 562 (1926), the Court held this principle of immunity to apply as well to State-owned commercial ships.

[6] AMERICAN LAW INSTITUTE, 1 RESTATEMENT OF THE LAW THIRD: THE FOREIGN RELATIONS LAW OF THE UNITED STATES 391 (1987).

[7] The Acting Legal Adviser of the Department of State, Jack B. Tate, stated in a letter to the Acting Attorney General that in future cases the Department would follow the restrictive principle. 26 Department of State Bulletin 984 (1952). Previously, when a case against a foreign State arose, the State Department routinely asked the Department of Justice to inform the court that the government favored the principle of absolute immunity; and the courts usually acceded to this advice. The Tate letter meant that the government would no longer make this suggestion in cases against foreign States involving commercial activity.

[8] 28 U.S.C. §§ 1602-11.

[9] Id. § 1604.

[10] Id. § 1605.

[11] Id. § 1610.

[12] P.L. 104-132, Title II, § 221 (April 24, 1976); 110 Stat. 1241; 28 U.S.C. § 1605(a)(7).

[13] Id.

[14] The State Department identifies State sponsors of terrorism pursuant to § 6(j) of the Export Administration Act of 1979 (50 App. U.S.C. § 2405(j)), § 620A of the Foreign Assistance Act (22 U.S.C. § 2371), and § 40(d) of the Arms Export Control Act (22 U.S.C. § 2780(d)). The list, which is published annually, currently includes Cuba, Iran, North Korea, Sudan, and Syria. See 22 CFR §126.1(a) (2002). Iraq and Libya are no longer designated State sponsors of terrorism. The White House gave notice on June 26, 2008, that North Korea will lose its designation after the 45-day waiting period provided by statute. See U.S. Department of State, Fact Sheet: North Korea: Presidential Action on State Sponsor of Terrorism (SST) and the Trading with the Enemy Act (TWEA)(June 26, 2008), available at [http://www.state.gov/r/pa/prs/ps/2008/jun/106281.htm].

[15] As initially enacted, the statute provided that a terrorist State could not be sued if "either the claimant or victim was not a U.S. national." Concern that the provision could be read to require that both the claimant and victim be U.S. nationals, which might have excluded some of the families injured by the terrorist bombing of Pan Am 103 over Lockerbie, Scotland, led Congress to amend the language in 1997 to bar such suits only if "neither the claimant nor the victim was a national of the United States...." See P.L. 105-11; H.Rept. 105-48 (April 10, 1997).

[16] 28 U.S.C. § 1605 note.

[17] Id. § 1610(b)(2). These amendments to the FSIA did not receive much debate or explanation during the AEDPA's consideration by the Senate and the House. Provisions similar to what was enacted were included in both the Senate and the House measures as introduced (S. 735, § 221 and H.R. 2703, § 803, respectively). But no committee report was filed on either bill; and the only change that appears to have been made during floor debate was a slight amendment by Representative Hyde in a manager's amendment in the House imposing a 10-year statute of limitations on such suits and slightly modifying the provision concerning pre-trial arbitration. See 142 CONG. REC. H2164 (daily ed., March 13, 1996). The report of the conference committee simply stated as follows: Section 221 — House section 803 recedes to Senate section 206, with modifications. This subtitle provides that nations designated as state sponsors of terrorism under section 6(j) of the Export Administration Act of 1979 will be amenable to suit in U.S. courts for terrorist acts. It permits U.S. federal courts to hear claims seeking money damages for personal injury or death against such nations and arising from terrorist acts they commit, or direct to be committed, against American citizens or nationals outside of the foreign state's territory, and for such acts within the state's territory if the state involved has refused to arbitrate the claim. H.Rept. 104-518 (1996). However, the House had adopted a similar measure during the second session of the previous Congress (H.R. 934). The Department of State and the Department of Justice had opposed the legislation at that time. The House Judiciary Committee explained the rationale of the bill as follows: The difficulty U.S. citizens have had in obtaining remedies for torture and other injuries suffered abroad illustrates the need for remedial legislation. A foreign sovereign violates international law if it practices torture, summary execution, or genocide. Yet under current law a U.S. citizen who is tortured or killed abroad cannot sue the foreign sovereign in U.S. courts, even when the foreign country wrongly refuses to hear the citizen's case. Therefore, in some instances a U.S. citizen

who was tortured (or the family of one who was murdered) will be without a remedy. H.R. 934 stands for the principle that U.S. citizens who are grievously mistreated abroad should have an effective remedy for damages in some tribunal, either in the country where the mistreatment occurred or in the United States. To this end, the bill would add a new exception to the FSIA that would allow suits against foreign sovereigns that subject U.S. citizens to torture, extrajudicial killings or genocide and do not provide adequate remedies for those harms. H.Rept. 103-702, 103rd Cong., 2d Sess. (August 16, 1994), at 4.

[18] See Flatow v. Islamic Republic of Iran, 999 F. Supp. 1 (D.D.C. 1998). The FSIA exception creates jurisdiction over the defendant State, making it amenable to lawsuits based on causes of action established elsewhere in law, just as they would apply to private persons and entities, but does not create a private right of action.

[19] P.L. 104-208, Title I, §101(c) (September 30, 1996), 110 Stat. 3009-172; codified at 28 U.S.C. § 1605 note (see supra note 3).

[20] The provision appears to have first arisen in the House-Senate conference committee on H.R. 3610. See H.Rept. 104-863, 104th Cong., 2d Sess. (September 28, 1996).

[21] 28 U.S.C. § 1608(e).

[22] See Alejandre v. Republic of Cuba, 996 F.Supp. 1239 (S.D. Fla. 1997) ($50 million in compensatory damages and $137.7 million in punitive damages awarded to the families of three of the four persons who were killed when Cuban aircraft shot down two Brothers to the Rescue planes in 1996); Flatow v. Islamic Republic of Iran, 999 F. Supp. 1 (D.D.C. 1998) ($27 million in compensatory damages and $225 million in punitive damages awarded to the father of Alisa Flatow, who was killed in 1995 by a car bombing in the Gaza Strip by Islamic Jihad, an organization which the court found to be funded by Iran); and Cicippio v. Islamic Republic of Iran, 18 F. Supp. 2d 62 (D.D.C. 1998) ($65 million awarded in compensatory damages to three persons (and two of their spouses) who were kidnaped, held hostage, and tortured in Lebanon in the mid-1980s by Hezbollah, an organization which the court found to be funded by Iran).

[23] The Iran-U.S. Claims Tribunal at the Hague was created pursuant to provisions in the Algiers Accords of 1981 that led to the release of the U.S. hostages. Claims by U.S. nationals against Iran that were outstanding at the time of the release of the hostages as well as claims by Iranian nationals against the United States and contractual claims between the two governments were made subject to case-by-case arbitration by the Tribunal.

Most Iranian assets held by U.S. persons or entities at that time were transferred to the Federal Reserve Bank of New York and were either returned to Iran or were forwarded to an escrow account for use in satisfying judgments rendered against Iran by this Tribunal. See the various agreements between the United States and Iran relating to the release of the hostages (known as the Algiers Accords), 20 ILM 223-240 (January 1981); Executive Orders 12276-12284, 46 Fed. Reg. 7913 (January 19, 1981); and 31 CFR Part 535.

[24] 23 UST 3227 (1972).

[25] 21 UST 77 (1969).

[26] Flatow v. Islamic Republic of Iran, 74 F. Supp. 2d 18 (D.D.C. 1999) (quashing a writ of attachment for U.S. Treasury funds) and Flatow v. Islamic Republic of Iran, 76 F. Supp. 2d 16 (D.D.C. 1999) (quashing writs of attachment for Iran's embassy and chancery and two bank accounts holding proceeds from the rental of these properties). For a more detailed description of these proceedings, see Sean Murphy, Satisfaction of U.S. Judgments Against State Sponsors of Terrorism, 94 AM. J. INT'L L. 117 (2000).

[27] See Appendix B for a list of the amounts of the assets of each State on the terrorist list that are blocked in the U.S.

[28] 50 U.S.C. §§ 1701 et seq. IEEPA gives the President substantial authority to regulate economic transactions with foreign countries and nationals to deal with "any unusual and extraordinary threat, which has its source in whole or substantial part outside the United States, to the national security, foreign policy, or economy of the United States, if the President declares a national emergency with respect to such a threat."

[29] Executive Order 12170, 44 Fed. Reg. 65,729 (November 14, 1979).

[30] 50 U.S.C. App. § 5. TWEA, originally enacted in 1917, gives the President powers similar to those of IEEPA to regulate economic transactions with foreign countries and nationals in time of war. At the time it was used to freeze Cuba's assets in 1962, it also applied in times of national emergency; but that authority was eliminated when IEEPA was enacted in 1977. Sanctions previously imposed under that authority, however, were grandfathered. See 50 U.S.C. § 1708.

[31] In the 1960s, for instance, Congress directed the Foreign Claims Settlement Commission to determine the number and amount of legitimate claims against Cuba resulting from Fidel Castro's takeover of the government and subsequent expropriation of property from January 1, 1959, and October 16, 1964. P.L. 88-666, Title V (October 16, 1964), 73 Stat. 1110, codified at 22

Suits Against Terrorist States by Victims of Terrorism 65

U.S.C. § 1643. The program was completed in 1972 and found 5,911 claims totaling $1,851,057,358 (in 1972 valuations) to be valid. Those claims remain pending. In the Iran Claims Settlement Act of 1985, Congress directed the Foreign Claims Settlement Commission to determine the validity and amount of small claims against Iran (those for less than $250,000) pending at the time of the hostage crisis and to distribute to such claimants the proceeds of any en bloc settlement concluded by the U.S. and Iran. See P.L. 99-93, Title V, §§ 505-505 (August 16, 1985), 99 Stat. 437, codified at 50 U.S.C. § 1701 note. The United States and Iran concluded such an agreement in 1990. See State Department Office of the Legal Adviser, Cumulative Digest of United States Practice in International Law 1981-1988 (Book III) (1995), at 3201. All other pre-1981 claims against Iran (and against the United States by Iran and Iranian nationals) remained subject to case-by-case arbitrationby the Iran-U.S. Claims Tribunal.

[32] Both Cuba and Iran have reportedly enacted statutes allowing suits against the United States for acts of terrorism or "interference," and several substantial judgments against the United States have been handed down pursuant to those statutes. See infra at 54.

[33] P.L. 105-277, Div. A, Title I, § 117 (October 21, 1998), 112 Stat. 2681-491, codified at 28 U.S.C. § 1610(f)(1)(A). This section was added to the FSIA by § 117 of the Treasury and General Government Appropriations Act for Fiscal Year 1999, as contained in the Omnibus Consolidated and Emergency Supplemental Appropriations Act for Fiscal Year 1999, P.L. 105-277 (1998), 112 Stat. 2681. The provision, without the waiver authority, had originated in the Senate version of the Treasury appropriations bill; but the Senate Appropriations Committee had offered no explanation. See S. 2312 (105th Cong.) and S.Rept. 105-251(1998). It had also been offered during House floor debate on the House version of the Treasury appropriations bill by Representative Saxton but had been subject to a point of order as legislation on an appropriations bill. 144 CONG. REC. 15,856-59 (1998). In conference with the House, the provision was retained, but waiver authority for the President was added. The conference reports offered no further explanation. See H.R. 4104, H.Rept. 105-760 (1998), and H.Rept. 105-789 (1998). H.R. 4104 was not enacted but its provisions were folded into the omnibus act. Both immediately prior and after the enactment of the omnibus act, several members of the House and Senate expressed the view that the waiver authority of § 117 should be read to apply only to the requirement that the State and Justice Departments assist judgment creditors in locating the assets of terrorist States. See, e.g., 144 CONG. REC. 17,192-

93 (1998) (statements of Sen. Graham and Sen. Faircloth); id. at 27,742-43 (1998) (remark by Representative Pascrell); id. at 27,749-80 (remarks by Representative Meek, Representative Forbes, Representative Wolf, Representative Istook, Representative Northup, and Representative Aderholt); id. at 27,204 (remark by Representative Saxton). But at least one House member also expressed the view that the waiver authority applied to the whole of § 117. See 144 CONG. REC. 27,325 (1998).

[34] 28 U.S.C. § 1610(f)(1)(A).

[35] Presidential Determination 99-1 (October 21, 1998), reprinted in 34 WEEKLY COMP. PRES. DOC. 2088 (October 26, 1998). On the day the President exercised the waiver authority, the White House Office of the Press Secretary issued the following explanatory statement: ...[T]he struggle to defeat terrorism would be weakened, not strengthened, by putting into effect a provision of the Omnibus Appropriations Act for FY 1999. It would permit individuals who win court judgments against nations on the State Department's terrorist list to attach embassies and certain other properties of foreign nations, despite U.S. laws and treaty obligations barring such attachment. The new law allows the President to waive the provision in the national security interest of the United States. President Clinton has signed the bill and, in the interests of protecting America's security, has exercised the waiver authority. If the U.S. permitted attachment of diplomatic properties, then other countries could retaliate, placing our embassies and citizens overseas at grave risk. Our ability to use foreign properties as leverage in foreign policy disputes would also be undermined. Statement by the Press Secretary (October 21, 1998).

[36] Statement by President William J. Clinton Upon Signing H.R. 4328, 34 WEEKLY COMP. PRES. DOC. 2108 (November 2, 1998), reprinted in 1998 U.S.C.C.A.N. 576.

[37] The parties in both the Alejandre and the Flatow suits sought to persuade the courts that the President's waiver authority did not extend to the diplomatic properties and blocked assets of Cuba and Iran, but those efforts ultimately proved unavailing. See Alejandre v. Republic of Cuba, 42 F. Supp. 2d 1317 (S.D. Fla. 1999) (Presidential waiver authority held to apply only to the requirement that the Departments of State and Treasury assist judgment creditors and not to the provision subjecting blocked assets, including diplomatic property, to attachment). This decision was eventually reversed on other grounds by the U.S. Court of Appeals for the Eleventh Circuit — Alejandre v. Telefonica Larga Distancia de Puerto Rico, 183 F.3d 1277 (11th Cir. 1999). A decision by a federal district court in the Flatow

litigation construed the President's waiver authority broadly. See Flatow v. Islamic Republic of Iran, 76 F. Supp. 2d 16 (D.D.C. 1999); see also Jacobsen v. Oliver, 451 F. Supp. 2d 181, 189 (D.D.C. 2006) (waiver was effective for subsection (b), which would have authorized the award of punitive damages against foreign States).

[38] See Hearing Before the Senate Judiciary Committee on Terrorism: Victims' Access to Terrorists' Assets, 106th Congress, 1st Sess. (October 27, 1999) and Hearing Before the Subcommittee on Immigration and Claims of the House Judiciary Committee on H.R. 3485, the "Justice for Victims of Terrorists Act," 106th Congress, 2d Sess. (April 13, 2000).

[39] P.L. 106-386, § 2002 (October 28, 2000), 114 Stat. 1541.

[40] See, e.g., Anderson v. Islamic Republic of Iran, 90 F. Supp. 2d 107 (D.D.C. March 24, 2000) ($41.2 million in compensatory damages and $300 million in punitive damages awarded to a journalist who was kidnaped and held in deplorable conditions for seven years by Hezbollah, which the court found to be funded by Iran) and Eisenfeld v. Islamic Republic of Iran, 172 F. Supp. 2d 1 (D.D.C. July 11, 2000) ($24.7 million in compensatory damages and $300 million in punitive damages awarded to the families of two young Americans who were killed when a bomb placed by Hamas operatives exploded on the bus on which they were riding in Israel).

[41] See Murphy, supra note 26.

[42] Terrorism: Victims' Access to Terrorist Assets — Hearing Before the Senate Committee on the Judiciary, 106th Cong., 1st Sess. (October 27, 1999) (S. 106-941) (statement of Sen. Mack); Justice for Victims of Terrorism Act: Hearing Before the Subcommittee on Immigration and Claims of the House Committee on the Judiciary, 106th Cong., 2d Sess. (April 13, 2000) (statement of Representative McCollum) (expressing concern "that the President has exercised what was intended to be a narrow national security waiver too broadly, and stating that "[r]ather than waging a war on terrorism, it appears the administration is fighting the victims of terrorism").

[43] See id. (statements of Stephen Flatow and Maggie Alejandre Khuly).

[44] Id. (statement submitted by Treasury Deputy Secretary Eizenstat, Defense Under Secretary for Policy Slocombe, and State Under Secretary Pickering). Deputy Secretary Eizenstat had given similar testimony in the Senate hearing as well.

[45] H.Rept. 106-733, at 4 (2000). As initially reported, H.R. 3485 also amended the "PayGo" provision of the Balanced Budget and Emergency Deficit Control Act of 1985 (2 U.S.C. § 902(d)) to bar the Office of Management

and Budget from estimating any changes in direct spending outlays and receipts that would result from enactment of the bill. Because this provision apparently had not been discussed in committee, the committee subsequently deleted it before the bill went to the floor. See H.Rept. 106-733 (Part 2) (2000).

[46] 146 CONG. REC. H6938 (daily ed. July 25, 2000).

[47] P.L. 106-386, § 2002(f)(1) (October 28, 2000); 114 Stat. 1543. The statute primarily addresses the issue of international trafficking in women and children.

[48] These six cases are as follows: Higgins v. Islamic Republic of Iran, No. 1:99CV00377 (D.D.C. 2000) ($55.4 million in compensatory damages and $300 million in punitive damages awarded to the wife of a Marine colonel who was kidnaped and subsequently hanged by Hezbollah while serving as part of the United Nations Truce Supervision Organization in Lebanon); Sutherland v. Islamic Republic of Iran, 151 F. Supp. 2d 27 (D.D.C. 2001) ($46.5 million in compensatory damages and $300 million in punitive damages awarded to a professor (and his family) who was kidnaped while teaching at the American University in Beirut and subsequently imprisoned in "horrific and inhumane conditions" for six and a half years by Hezbollah); Jenco v. Islamic Republic of Iran, 154 F. Supp. 2d 27 (D.D.C. 2001) ($14.6 million in compensatory damages and $300 million in punitive damages awarded to the estate and family of a priest who was kidnaped while working in Beirut as the Director of Catholic Relief Services and imprisoned in terrible conditions for a year and a half by Hezbollah); Polhill v. Islamic Republic of Iran, 2001 U.S.Dist.LEXIS 15322 (D.D.C. 2001) ($31.5 million in compensatory damages and $300 million in punitive damages awarded to the family of an American citizen who was kidnapped while working as a professor in Beirut and held in "deplorable" conditions for more than three years by Hezbollah); Wagner v. Islamic Republic of Iran, 172 F. Supp. 2d 128 (D.D.C. 2001) ($16.3 million in compensatory damages and $300 million in punitive damages awarded to the estate and family of a petty officer in the U.S. Navy who was killed by a car bomb driven by a Hezbollah suicide bomber); and Stethem v. Islamic Republic of Iran, 201 F. Supp. 2d 78 (D.D.C. 2002) ($21.2 million in compensatory damages awarded to the family of a serviceman who was tortured and killed during the hijacking of a TWA plane in 1985, $8 million awarded in compensatory damages to six servicemen and their families for their torture and detention during and after the same hijacking, and $300 million in punitive damages awarded against Iran for its recruitment, training, and

financing of Hezbollah, the terrorist group the court found to be responsible for the hijacking). It might be noted that in Stethem only the award to the Stethem family was originally covered by § 2002 of the Victims of Trafficking Act; the second suit filed by the six servicemen and their families — Carlson v. Islamic Republic of Iran — which was consolidated with Stethem was not covered by § 2002 but was later added to the list of compensable suits by P.L. 107-228 (September 30, 2002).

[49] See Murphy, supra note 26, at 138.

[50] A Foreign Military Sales Fund is a Treasury holding account established to facilitate the sale of military items to foreign countries or international organizations, pursuant to the Arms Control Export Act, 22 U.S.C. § 2751 et seq. Foreign purchasers place monies in the fund under individual sub-accounts from which the Department of Defense pays for military equipment and services provided to the purchaser by DoD or private suppliers.

[51] Congress provided $1.353 billion in 1979 to pay for four DDG-993 destroyers Iran had ordered but that became available for the U.S. Navy after the revolution in Iran led to the termination of the contract. P.L. 96-38 (July 25, 1979), 93 Stat. 97, 99; S.Rept. 96-224 at 25.

[52] Paragraph (1) is codified at 28 U.S.C. § 1610(f)(1) and the modified waiver authority is codified at 28 U.S.C. § 1610(f)(3). It applies to "property with respect to which financial transactions are prohibited or regulated pursuant to [IEEPA, TWEA, or any other law or regulation]."

[53] Presidential Determination No. 2001-03 (October 28, 2000); 65 Fed. Reg. 66,483.

[54] While the statute itself made no express mention of how the waiver was meant to be executed, the report of the House-Senate conference committee on the "Victims of Trafficking" bill expressed an intent that the waiver authority of § 2002 be exercised only on a case-by-case basis, as follows: Subsection 1(f) of this bill repeals the waiver authority granted in Section 117 of the Treasury and General Government Appropriations Act for fiscal year 1999, replacing it with a clearer but narrower waiver authority in the underlying statute. The Committee hopes clarity in the legislative history and intent of subsection 1(f), in the context of the section as a whole, will ensure appropriate application of the new waiver authority. The Committee's intent is that the President will review each case when the court issues a final judgement to determine whether to use the national security waiver, whether to help the plaintiffs collect from a foreign state's non-blocked assets in the United States, whether to allow the courts to

attach and execute against blocked assets, or whether to use existing authorities to vest and pay those assets as damages to the victims of terrorism. When a future President does make a decision whether to invoke the waiver, he should consider seriously whether the national security standard for a waiver has been met. In enacting this legislation, Congress is expressing the view that the attachment and execution of frozen assets to enforce judgements in cases under the Anti-Terrorism Act of 1996 is not by itself contrary to the national security interest. Indeed, in the view of the Committee, it is generally in the national security interest of the United States to make foreign state sponsors of terrorism pay court-awarded damages to American victims, so neither the Foreign Sovereign Immunities Act nor any other law will stand in the way of justice. Thus, in the view of the committee the waiver authority should not be exercised in a routine or blanket manner, but only where U.S. national security interests would be implicated in taking action against particular blocked assets or where alternative recourse — such as vesting and paying those assets — may be preferable to court attachment. H.Rept. 106-939, at 117-118 (2000).

[55] 65 Fed. Reg. 70,382 (November 22, 2000) and 65 Fed. Reg. 78,533 (December 15, 2000).

[56] The original judgment had been rendered in Alejandre v. Republic of Cuba, 996 F. Supp. 1239 (S.D. Fla. 1997).

[57] See the six cases summarized supra, note 48.

[58] Other default judgments against Iran that were handed down after the enactment of § 2002 on October 28, 2000, and prior to the adjournment of the 107th Congress in late 2002, but that were not covered by § 2002, included Elahi v. Islamic Republic of Iran, 124 F. Supp. 2d 97 (D.D.C. 2000) ($11.7 million in compensatory damages and $300 million in punitive damages awarded to the administrator of the estate of an Iranian dissident and naturalized U.S. citizen killed by gunshot in Paris by the Iranian Ministry of Information and Security); Mousa v. Islamic Republic of Iran, 238 F. Supp. 2d 1 (D.D.C. 2001) ($12 million in compensatory damages and $120 million in punitive damages awarded to woman who suffered severe and long-lasting injuries from a suicide bombing of a bus in Jerusalem carried out at the instigation of Hamas, an entity the court found to be supported by Iran); Hegna v. Islamic Republic of Iran, No. 1:00CV00716 (D.D.C. 2002) ($42 million in damages awarded to the family of a U.S. Agency for International Development officer who was killed by Hezbollah militants during a hijacking of a Kuwaiti Airlines flight in 1984); Weinstein v. Islamic Republic of Iran, 184 F. Supp. 2d 13 (D.D.C.

2002) ($33 million in compensatory damages and $150 million in punitive damages awarded to the family and estate of a person who was severely injured in a bus bombing in Jerusalem carried out by Hamas, which the court found to be funded by Iran, and who subsequently died from those injuries); Cronin v. Islamic Republic of Iran, 238 F. Supp. 2d 222 (D.D.C. 2002) ($1.2 million in compensatory damages and $300 million in punitive damages awarded to an individual who, while he was a graduate student in Lebanon in 1984, was kidnaped and tortured for four days by Hezbollah and two other paramilitary groups which the court found to have been organized, funded, trained, and controlled by Iran); and Surette v. Islamic Republic of Iran, 231 F. Supp. 2d 260 (D.D.C. 2002) ($18.96 million in compensatory damages and $300 million in punitive damages awarded to the widow and sister of CIA agent William Buckley who was kidnaped in Beirut and tortured for 14 months by the Islamic Jihad, an entity the court found to be organized and funded by Iran, and who ultimately died while in captivity). In addition, two default judgments were handed down against Iraq — Daliberti v. Republic of Iraq, 146 F. Supp. 2d 19 (D.D.C. 2001) ($12.8 million in compensatory damages awarded to four U.S. citizens who were detained and tortured for varying periods of time between 1992 and 1995 by Iraq and $6 million awarded to their spouses) and Hill v. Republic of Iraq, 175 F. Supp. 2d 36 (D.D.C. 2001) ($9 million in compensatory damages against Iraq and Saddam Hussein and $300 million in punitive damages against Saddam Hussein personally awarded to twelve U.S. citizens who were held in hostage status by Iraq after its invasion of Kuwait in 1990). See infra note 134 (definition of "hostage status"). In the Hill case, the court subsequently found that an additional 168 plaintiffs had established their right to relief for being held hostage by Iraq; and the court awarded them approximately $85 million in compensatory damages. See Hill v. Republic of Iraq, 2003 U.S. Dist. LEXIS 3725 (D.D.C. 2003).

[59] See Shawn Zeller, Hoping to Thaw Those Frozen Funds, 33 NAT'L J. 3368-69 (October 27, 2001).

[60] P.L. 107-77 (November 28, 2001). The text of the act and the conference report (H.Rept. 107-278) is printed at 147 CONG. REC. H7986-H8038 (daily ed. November 9, 2001).

[61] Id. § 626, reprinted at 147 CONG. REC. H8001 (daily ed. September 13, 2001).

[62] See 147 CONG. REC. S9365 (daily ed. September 13, 2001). The Hollings amendment generally followed the scheme of § 2002 by specifying the filing dates of four of the five additional cases rather than identifying them

by name. The specified dates were May 17, 1996; May 7, 1997; October 22, 1999; and December 15, 1999. It identified the Roeder case only by its filing number in the federal district court in the District of Columbia — Case Number 1:00CV03110 (ESG). For the text of the amendment, see 147 CONG. REC. S9398-9400 (daily ed. September 13, 2001).

[63] H.Rept. 107-278 (2001), reprinted at 147 CONG. REC. H 8033 (daily ed. November 9, 2001).

[64] Office of the White House Press Secretary, "President Signs Commerce Appropriations Bill: Statement by the President on H.R. 2500" (November 28, 2001), available on the White House website.

[65] P.L. 107-228, § 686 (September 30, 2002). Various members of Congress had previously introduced bills to add suits to the list compensable under § 2002. See, e.g., H.R. 4647 (107th Cong.).

[66] Civil Action No. 00-1309 (D.D.C., filed June 6, 2000).

[67] Civil Action No. 00-0159 (D.D.C., filed January 28, 2000).

[68] Stethem v. The Islamic Republic of Iran and Carlson v. The Islamic Republic of Iran, 201 F. Supp. 2d 78 (D.D.C. 2002).

[69] As with the other suits included within § 2002, the Carlson suit is not specified by name but merely by its filing date of June 6, 2000. The amendment, sponsored by Representative Manzullo, was part of a group of amendments adopted by voice vote on May 16, 2001. See 147 CONG. REC. H2224-H2239 (daily ed. May 16, 2001).

[70] P.L. 107-297 (November 26, 2002), 116 Stat. 2322.

[71] The term "blocked asset" is defined in § 201(d) of TRIA to mean (A) any asset seized or frozen by the United States under [TWEA or IEEPA]; and (B) does not include property that —(I) is subject to a license issued by the United States Government for final payment, transfer, or disposition by or to a person subject to the jurisdiction of the United States in connection with a transaction for which the issuance of such license has been specifically required by statute other than [IEEPA] or the United Nations Participation Act of 1945 (22 U.S.C. 287 et seq.); or (ii) in the case of property subject to the Vienna Convention on Diplomatic Relations or the Vienna Convention on Consular Relations, or that enjoys equivalent privileges and immunities under the law of the United States, is being used exclusively for diplomatic or consular purposes.

[72] The Director, Office of Foreign Assets Control determined that the total compensable awards exceeded 90 percent of the available funds as of June 3, 2003, and directed his office to propose an appropriate pro rata distribution for Iran-related applications that were received by April 7,

2003. See Memorandum, Department of the Treasury, Determination of Insufficiency of Funds Victims of Trafficking and Violence Protection Act of 2000, Public Law No. 106-386, as Amended (June 3, 2003), available at [http://www.treasury.gov/offices/enforcement/ofac/legal/notices/insf_funds.pdf]. All judgment creditors of Iran eligible for compensation under § 2002 have received their payments.

[73] The proposal used as its standard the amount available to the families of public safety officers who are killed in the line of duty under subpart 1 of part L of title I of the Omnibus Crime Control and Safe Streets Act of 1968, 42 U.S.C. §§ 3796 et seq. That act originally set the death benefit at $50,000; in 2001 Congress increased the death benefit to $250,000, adjusted annually for inflation. See P.L. 107-56, § 613(a) (October 26, 2001); 115 Stat. 369.

[74] Benefits for U.S. Victims of International Terrorism: Hearing Before the Senate Committee on Foreign Relations, 108th Cong. (July 17, 2003).

[75] Flatow v. Islamic Republic of Iran, 999 F. Supp. 1, 26 (D.D.C. 1998).

[76] Punitive damages were previously available only with respect to agencies and instrumentalities of foreign governments. The FSIA provision for liability and damages is 22 U.S.C. § 1606: As to any claim for relief with respect to which a foreign state is not entitled to immunity under section 1605 or 1607 of this chapter, the foreign state shall be liable in the same manner and to the same extent as a private individual under like circumstances; but a foreign state except for an agency or instrumentality thereof shall not be liable for punitive damages; if, however, in any case wherein death was caused, the law of the place where the action or omission occurred provides, or has been construed to provide, for damages only punitive in nature, the foreign state shall be liable for actual or compensatory damages measured by the pecuniary injuries resulting from such death which were incurred by the persons for whose benefit the action was brought.

[77] Cicippio-Puleo v. Iran, 353 F.3d 1024 (D.C. Cir. 2004), cert. denied, 544 U.S. 1010 (2005).

[78] See 28 U.S.C. § 1603(b) (defining "agencies and instrumentalities").

[79] 353 F.3d at 1034.

[80] Cicippio v. Islamic Republic of Iran, 18 F. Supp. 2d 62 (D.D.C. 1998).

[81] 353 F.3d at 1029 (agreeing that, "insofar as the Flatow Amendment creates a private right of action against officials, employees, and agents of foreign states, the cause of action is limited to claims against those officials in their individual, as opposed to their official, capacities) (emphasis in original).

[82] Id at 1030. The government responded that Neither Section 1605(a)(7) nor the Flatow Amendment, nor the two considered in tandem, offers any indication that Congress intended to take the more provocative step of creating a private right of action against foreign governments themselves. Such a move could have serious adverse consequences for the conduct of foreign relations by the Executive Branch, and therefore an intent to do so should not be inferred - it should be recognized only if Congress has acted clearly in that direction.

[83] Cicippio-Puleo v. Islamic Republic of Iran, Case No. 01-01496 (D.D.C. 2005).

[84] 353 F.3d at 1034.

[85] Id. (citing Kentucky v. Graham, 473 U.S. 159, 165 (1985)).

[86] See, e.g., Bodoff v. Islamic Republic of Iran, 424 F. Supp. 2d 74 (D.D.C. 2006) (Lamberth, J.) (awarding estate of terrorist victim $300 million in punitive damages against Ayotollah Khamanei); Hausler v. Republic of Cuba, No. 02-12475 CA 01 (Miami-Dade Co., Fla., 11th Cir. Ct., decided January 19, 2007) (awarding $300 million in punitive damages against same defendants); Weininger v. Republic of Cuba, No. 03-22920 CA 20 (Miami-Dade Co., Fla., 11th Cir. Ct. decided November 11, 2004) (awarding $65 million in punitive damages against Fidel Castro and Raul Castro, as individuals and as agencies and instrumentalitities of Cuba and the Cuban army as an agency and instrumentality).

[87] Pugh v. Libya, Civil Action No. 02-02026, 2008 WL 134220 (D.D.C. 2008) (awarding treble damages — $5.268 billion — against six Libyan agents); Hurst v. Libya, 474 F. Supp. 2d 19, 29 (D.D.C. 2007) ("An official may be sued in one's personal capacity for actions taken in one's official capacity without destroying sovereign immunity.").

[88] See, e.g., Dammarell v. Islamic Republic of Iran, 370 F. Supp. 2d 218, 220-21 (D.D.C. 2005) (requiring plaintiffs to amend their complaint to plead specific causes of action under the common law or statutes of their respective home states).

[89] Peterson v. Islamic Republic of Iran, 515 F. Supp. 2d 25, 46 (D.D.C. 2007).

[90] Rux v. Republic of Sudan, 495 F. Supp. 2d 541 (E.D. Va. 2007). Relatives who had not been financially dependant on the decedents were unable to recover damages. See id at 566-68.

[91] Death on the High Seas Act, 41 Stat. 537, 46 U.S.C. app. §§ 761-67.

[92] Case Number 1:00CV03110 (ESG) (D.D.C., filed December 29, 2000).

[93] The Algiers Accords contain the following provision: ... [T]he United States ... will thereafter bar and preclude the prosecution against Iran of any

pending or future claim of the United States or a United States national arising out of events occurring before the date of this declaration related to (A) the seizure of the 52 United States nationals on Nov. 4, 1979, (B) their subsequent detention, (C) injury to United States property or property of the United States nationals within the United States embassy compound in Tehran after Nov. 3, 1979, and (D) injury to the United States nationals or their property as a result of popular movements in the course of the Islamic Revolution in Iran which were not an act of the Government of Iran. The United States will also bar and preclude the prosecution against Iran in the courts of the United States of any pending or future claims asserted by persons other than the United States nationals arising out of the events specified in the preceding sentence. 20 ILM 227 (1981).

[94] P.L. 107-77, Title VI, § 626(c) (November 28, 2001), amending 28 U.S.C. § 1605(a)(7)(A).
[95] H.Rept. 107-278 (2001).
[96] Statement on Signing the Departments of Commerce, Justice, and State, the Judiciary and Related Agencies Appropriations Act, 2002, 37 WEEKLY COMP. PRES. DOC. 1723, 1724 (November 28, 2001).
[97] The amendment inverted two letters in the case reference to Roeder that had been contained in P.L. 107-17, changing "1:00CV03110 (ESG)" to "1:00CV03110 (EGS)." See P.L. 107-117, Title II, § 208 (January 10, 2002). This technical correction had originally been included in the DOD appropriations bill as reported and adopted by the Senate but without explanation. See H.R. 3338 as reported by the Senate Appropriations Committee (S.Rept. 107-109 (2001)) and Senate floor debate at 147 CONG. REC. S12476-S12529 (daily ed. December 6, 2001), S12586-S12676 and S12779-S12812 (daily ed. December 7, 2001).
[98] H.Rept. 107-350 (2001).
[99] Remarks on Signing the Department of Defense and Emergency Supplemental Appropriations for Recovery from and Response to Terrorist Attacks on the United States Act, 2002, in Arlington, Virginia, 38 WEEKLY COMP. PRES. DOC. 44 (January 10, 2002).
[100] Roeder v. Islamic Republic of Iran, 195 F. Supp. 2d 140 (D.D.C. 2002).
[101] The court said that it did not have jurisdiction over the suit until Congress amended the FSIA by means of § 626(c) of the FY2002 appropriations act for the Departments of Justice, Commerce, and State, which was signed into law on November 28, 2001. Prior to that amendment, it said, the suit did not fall within the terrorist state exception to the FSIA because Iran had not been declared to be a terrorist state at the time it seized and held the

American personnel hostage. The court said also that, absent an "express statement of intent by Congress," it could not apply § 626(c) retroactively.

[102] The court stressed that the terrorist state exception which Congress had added to the FSIA in 1996 meant only that U.S. courts could exercise jurisdiction over such cases. Traditional State immunity, in other words, was eliminated as a jurisdictional barrier. But that amendment to the FSIA did not in itself, the court said, provide a cause of action for such suits. The specific statute providing for such a cause of action which Congress enacted later in 1996, it said, provided only for a cause of action against an official, employee, or agent of a terrorist State, not against the terrorist State itself. (See P.L. 104-208, Div. A, Title I, § 101(c) (September 30, 1996) ("Flatow Amendment"); 110 Stat. 3009-172; 28 U.S.C. § 1605 note; supra note 3.)

[103] The court stressed that an act of Congress "ought never to be considered to violate the law of nations, if any other possible construction remains." None of the statutes Congress had adopted relating to a cause of action generally or to Roeder itself, the court said, unambiguously declared an intent to override the Algiers Accords. Nor, it said, did they unambiguously declare an intent not to override the Accords. They, and their "scant" legislative history, were ambiguous on the question, it held, and, consequently, must be construed not to conflict with the Accords: Neither the Anti-Terrorism Act, the Flatow Amendment, Subsection 626(c), or Section 208 contain the type of express statutory mandate sufficient to abrogate an international executive agreement. Furthermore ..., the legislative histories of these statutes contain no clear statements of Congressional intent to specifically abrogate the Algiers Accords. Therefore, ... unless and until Congress expresses its clear intent to overturn the provisions of a binding agreement between two nations that has been in effect for over twenty years, this Court can not interpret these statutes to abrogate that agreement. Roeder v. Islamic Republic of Iran, supra, at 177. The court also rejected the argument that because the United States entered into the Algiers Accords under duress, the Accords constituted "an unenforceable illegal contract." "Whatever emotional appeal and rhetorical flourish this argument contains," the court said, "it is absolutely without basis in law." Id. at 168.

[104] The court did not base its decision on any separation of powers considerations. But it did say that if it had construed § 626(c) to apply retroactively, Congress's "post-judgment retroactive imposition of jurisdiction [would raise] serious separation of powers concerns" and might be "an impermissible encroachment by Congress into the sphere of the federal courts...." Id. at 161. "By expressly directing legislation at pending

litigation, Congress has arguably attempted to determine the outcome of this litigation," it said. Id. at 163. The court also suggested that the narrowness of Congress's enactments, i.e., their application only to this one case and not to any others, raised possible Article III concerns. Id. at 165-66.

[105] In commenting on what it called the "repeated ethical failures by class counsel," the court stated that "[p]laintiffs' counsel in this case repeatedly presented meritless arguments to this Court, repeatedly failed to substantiate their arguments by reference to any supporting authority, and repeatedly failed to bring to the Court's attention the existence of controlling authority that conflicted with those arguments." Id. at 185.

[106] Roeder v. The Islamic Republic of Iran, 333 F.3d 228, 238 (D.C. Cir. 2003) ("While legislative history may be useful in determining intent, the joint explanatory statements here go well beyond the legislative text of § 208, which did nothing more than correct a typographical error.").

[107] The court noted, but did not decide whether the amendments were an impermissible intrusion by Congress into the role of the courts. Id. at 237 and n.5.

[108] S.Rept. 107-218, at 167 (2002).

[109] H.J.Res. 2149 (108th Cong.); S. 762 (108th Cong.); S. 1689 (108th Cong.)

[110] E.O. 13290, 68 Fed. Reg. 14,305-08 (March 24, 2003).

[111] See Tom Schoenberg, Fights Loom for Iraqi Riches, LEGAL TIMES (March 31, 2003). Judgment creditors were paid about $140 million from the vested assets to cover the unsatisfied portions of judgments and interest. Judgments satisfied from Iraqi assets include Dadesho v. Government of Iraq, D.C. No. CV-92-05491-REC (E.D. Cal. 1995) ($1.5 million for 1990 foiled assassination plot), appeal dismissed, 139 F.3d 766 (9th Cir. 1998); Hill v. Republic of Iraq, 175 F. Supp. 2d 36 (D.D.C. 2001) ($94,110,000.00 in compensatory damages for civilians detained in Iraq); Daliberti v. Republic of Iraq, 146 F. Supp. 2d 19 (D.D.C. 2001) ($18,823,289.00 for civilian contractors held hostage in Iraq).

[112] P.L. 108-11, § 1503 (April 16, 2003).

[113] See Memorandum for the Secretary of State (Presidential Determination No. 2003-23) (May 7, 2003). This Determination simply replicated the general language of the Supplemental Appropriations Act provision. But in a subsequent message to Congress, President Bush stated: ... [B]y my memorandum to the Secretary of State and Secretary of Commerce of May 7, 2003, (Presidential Determination 2003-23), I made inapplicable with respect to Iraq section 620A of the Foreign Assistance Act of 1961, Public Law 87-195, as amended, and any other provision of law that applies to

countries that have supported terrorism. Such provisions of law that apply to countries that have supported terrorism include, but are not limited to, 28 U.S.C. 1605(a)(7), 28 U.S.C. 1610, and section 201 of the Terrorism Risk Insurance Act. President George Bush, Message to the Congress of the United States (May 22, 2003), available on the White House website.

[114] E.O. 13303, 68 Fed. Reg. 31,931 (May 28, 2003).

[115] Acree v. Republic of Iraq, 276 F. Supp. 2d 95 (D.D.C. 2003).

[116] Id. at 98.

[117] Acree v. Snow, 276 F. Supp. 2d 31 (D.D.C.), aff'd 78 Fed.Appx. 133 (D.C. Cir. 2003) (unpublished opinion); Smith v. Federal Reserve Bank of New York, 280 F. Supp. 2d 314 (S.D.N.Y), aff'd 346 F.3d 264 (2nd Cir. 2003) (attempted enforcement of default judgment of $64,002,483.19 against Iraq by plaintiff victims of September 11, 2001, terrorist attacks).

[118] 276 F. Supp. 2d at 33.

[119] Id.

[120] Acree v. Republic of Iraq, 370 F.3d 41 (D.C. Cir. 2004), cert. denied, 544 U.S. 1010 (2005).

[121] 353 F.3d 1024 (D.C. Cir. 2004).

[122] The court also applied the Cicippio-Puleo holding to affirm that the Flatow Amendment cause of action against officials, employees, and agents of foreign States, is limited to claims against those officials "in their individual, as opposed to their official, capacities." Id. at 1034. This was so, the court found, because "to construe the Flatow Amendment as permitting official-capacity claims would eviscerate the recognized distinction between suits against governments and suits against individual government officials." Id. (citing the U.S. brief filed as amicus curiae).

[123] 544 U.S. 1010 (2005).

[124] Acree v. Republic of Iraq, 2008 WL 2764858 (D.D.C. 2008). The court did not expressly consider the effect of § 1083 of the FY2008 NDAA or its waiver with respect to Iraq.

[125] H.Con.Res. 344 (108th Cong.).

[126] See P.L. 108-106, 117 Stat. 1209 (2003).

[127] Id. Presumably, the "17 plaintiffs in the [Acree case]" in H.R. 1321 meant those plaintiffs who were actually held prisoner, but would have excluded 37 family members and relatives, who also participated as plaintiffs and were awarded damages of from $5 - 10 million each. Acree v. Republic of Iraq, 271 F. Supp. 2d 179 (D.D.C. 2003), vacated by 370 F.3d 41 (D.C. Cir. 2004), cert. denied, 544 U.S. 1010 (2005).

[128] 262 F. Supp. 2d 217 (S.D.N.Y.2003).

[129] Id. at 228 (citing Nixon v. Fitzgerald, 457 U.S. 731, 749, 102 S.Ct. 2690, 73 L.Ed.2d 349 (1982) for the proposition that a claim against a U.S. president for the such conduct would be barred because of "the president's absolute immunity from damages for conduct associated with the exercise of his official duties").
[130] Id. at 232 (finding expert testimony sufficient).
[131] Smith v. Federal Reserve Bank of New York, 280 F. Supp. 2d 314 (S.D.N.Y), aff'd 346 F.3d 264 (2nd Cir. 2003). Section 201 of TRIA provides that "the blocked assets of [ajudgment debtor] terrorist party (including the blocked assets of any agency or instrumentality of that terrorist party) shall be subject to execution or attachment in aid of execution" of compensatory damages. See supra note 71 for TRIA § 201 definition of "blocked asset."
[132] 346 F.3d at 272.
[133] 175 F. Supp. 2d 36 (D.D.C. 2001).
[134] Congress defined "hostage status" in § 599C(d)(1) of P.L. 101-513, with respect to U.S. hostages in Iraq or Kuwait, as the status of being held "in custody by governmental or military authorities of a country or taking refuge within that country in fear of being taken into such custody (including residing in any diplomatic mission or consular post in the country)...." Congress allocated $10 million to pay the persons in hostage status "at the rate of pay for a position at GS-9 of the General Schedule for the period in which such hostages remained in a hostage status without the hostages (or their family members on their behalf) receiving salaries or wages from their employers." P.L. 101-513 § 599C(b)(2) and (e).
[135] The court found that It is beyond dispute that the American citizens denied permission to leave Kuwait and Iraq from August through mid-December, 1990, by the armed forces and civilian police of the Republic of Iraq were "hostages" within the meaning of the FSIA. 175 F. Supp. 2d. at 46.
[136] The court awarded the punitive damages against Saddam Hussein based on the assumption that he was "an agency or instrumentality" of Iraq, apparently without considering whether the FSIA definition of "agency or instrumentality" supports that view. See id. at 48.
[137] Hill v. Republic of Iraq, 2003 U.S. Dist. LEXIS 3725 (D.D.C. 2003).
[138] E.O. 13290, 68 Fed. Reg. 14,307 (March 20, 2003).
[139] Vine v. Republic of Iraq, 459 F. Supp. 2d 10 (2006).
[140] Immediately after Iraq's invasion of Kuwait, Saddam Hussein issued a directive prohibiting foreigners, which included some 2,000 Americans, from leaving Iraq or Kuwait. Subsequently, Saddam issued an order

directing foreigners to report to two hotels in Bagdad, from which they were relocated to strategic sites to act as "human shields." Many disobeyed the directive and sought refuge in safehouses and diplomatic properties. See Vine v. Republic of Iraq, 459 F. Supp. 2d 10, 11-15 (2006).

[141] Simon v. Republic of Iraq, Civ. No. 03-691 (D.D.C.).

[142] Seyam v. Republic of Iraq, 16 Civ. No. 03-888 (D.D.C.).

[143] 28 U.S.C. § 1605(f).

[144] 459 F. Supp. 2d at 21-22 (noting that the "D.C. Circuit has held that equitable tolling 'does not bring about an automatic extension of the statute of limitations by the length of the tolling period.'" (citing Phillips v. Heine, 984 F.2d 489, 492 (D.C. Cir. 1993)).

[145] Simon v. Republic of Iraq, 2008 WL 2497417 (D.C. Cir. 2008).

[146] 480 F. Supp. 2d 60 (D.D.C.), aff'd No. 07-7057 (D.C. Cir. 2007) (per curiam), petition for cert. filed (U.S. February 19, 2008) (No. 07-1090).

[147] Daliberti v. Republic of Iraq, 146 F. Supp. 2d 19 (D.D.C. 2001).

[148] 480 F. Supp. 2d at 70.

[149] Docket No. 07-1090.

[150] Lawton v. Iraq, Civil Action No. 02-0474 RBW/DAR (D.D.C. 2006).

[151] See Notification of the Veto of H.R. 1585, the National Defense Authorization Act for Fiscal Year 2008, H.R. DOC. NO. 110-88, available at [http://frwebgate.access.gpo.gov/cgibin/getdoc.cgi?dbname=110_cong_documentsanddocid=f:hd088.110]. The President predicted the following consequences: Immediately upon enactment, section 1083 would risk the freezing of substantial Iraqi assets in the United States — including those of the Development Fund for Iraq (DFI), the Central Bank of Iraq (CBI), and commercial entities in the United States in which Iraq has an interest. Section 1083 also would expose Iraq to new liability of at least several billion dollars by undoing judgments favorable to Iraq, by foreclosing available defenses on which Iraq is relying in pending litigation, and by creating a new Federal cause of action backed by the prospect of punitive damages to support claims that may previously have been foreclosed. This new liability, in turn, will only increase the potential for immediate entanglement of Iraqi assets in the United States. The aggregate financial impact of these provisions on Iraq would be devastating. Id. at 1.

[152] P.L. 110-181, § 1083(d).

[153] Id.

[154] Presidential Determination No. 2008-9 of January 28, 2008, Waiver of Section 1083 of the National Defense Authorization Act for Fiscal Year

2008, 73 Fed. Reg. 6,571 (2008)(waiving all provisions of § 1083 with respect to Iraq).

[155] White House Memorandum of Justification for Waiver of Section 1083 of the National Defense Authorization Act (January 28, 2008), available at [http://www.whitehouse.gov/news/releases/2008/01/20080128-12.html].

[156] Simon v. Republic of Iraq, 2008 WL 2497417 (D.C. Cir. 2008).

[157] It appears that the waiver of all of the provisions of § 1083 merely leaves the law as it was prior to the enactment of the NDAA with respect to claims against Iraq. Under Simon, plaintiffs with ongoing actions may continue to pursue them under 28 U.S.C. § 1605(a)(7) (as previously in force) and the Flatow Amendment, supplemented by state causes of action.

[158] Simon, slip op. at 3 (noting that "a statute that retroactively alters the consequences of primary conduct-as by 'impair[ing] rights a party possessed when he acted, increas[ing] a party's liability for past conduct, or impos[ing] new duties with respect to transactions already completed,'... is presumptively non-retroactive; such a statute applies to a pending case only if the Congress clearly so provides") (citing Landgraf v. USI Film Prods., 511 U.S. 244, 280 (1994)); id. at 4 (construing § 1083(c)-(d) of the NDAA). Specifically, the court noted that Congress, by specifying that "the amendments ... apply to any claim arising under section 1605A," must have meant to distinguish new claims from pending claims, inasmuch as "the amendments obviously would apply to any [claim under § 1605A)] and could apply to no other claim." Id.

[159] 28 U.S.C. § 1610 note (permitting the attachment of some blocked assets).

[160] Judgment holders would not be foreclosed from invoking other provisions for property attachment in the FSIA that were not amended by § 1083, if the creditors were able to locate assets that qualify for exceptions to sovereign immunity under those provisions. However, very few of these non-terrorism exceptions would likely apply. Iraqi property used for commercial activity in the United States would be attachable only if Iraq waives its immunity for that purpose, or if judgment stems from a claim that was also based on some commercial activity and the property is or was used for that activity. 28 U.S.C. § 1610(f) could potentially be used to satisfy outstanding terrorism judgments against Iraq against property regulated under an executive order issued pursuant to IEEPA, if the presidential waiver provided for in § 1610(f)(3), exercised by President Clinton in 2000, 28 U.S.C. § 1610 note, is somehow deemed to have lapsed or to be ineffective with respect to a particular asset. 28 U.S.C. § 1610(f)(2) also likely continues to apply. It provides, in pertinent part: At the request of any party in whose favor a

judgment has been issued with respect to a claim for which the foreign state is not immune under section 1605(a)(7) (as in effect before the enactment of section 1605A) or section 1605A, the Secretary of the Treasury and the Secretary of State should make every effort to fully, promptly, and effectively assist any judgment creditor or any court that has issued any such judgment in identifying, locating, and executing against the property of that foreign state or any agency or instrumentality of such state. (Amendments made by § 1083 emphasized).

[161] See supra notes 110-114 and accompanying text.

[162] 28 U.S.C. § 1610(a)(7) was amended by § 1083 to reflect the new section 28 U.S.C. § 1605A, but was not otherwise altered. Therefore, arguably, the waiver of § 1083 has no impact on assets sought to be attached to satisfy judgments against Iraq under previous 28 U.S.C. § 1605(a)(7).

[163] E.O. 13303, 68 Fed. Reg. 31,931 (May 28, 2003). Section 1 states: Unless licensed or otherwise authorized pursuant to this order, any attachment, judgment, decree, lien, execution, garnishment, or other judicial process is prohibited, and shall be deemed null and void, with respect to the following: (a) the Development Fund for Iraq, and (b) all Iraqi petroleum and petroleum products, and interests therein, and proceeds, obligations, or any financial instruments of any nature whatsoever arising from or related to the sale or marketing thereof, and interests therein, in which any foreign country or a national thereof has any interest, that are in the United States, that hereafter come within the United States, or that are or hereafter come within the possession or control of United States persons.

[164] The Administration could continue to argue that Presidential Determination No. 2003-23 (May 7, 2003), making certain anti-terrorism sanctions inapplicable with respect to Iraq (see supra note 113) pursuant to § 1503 of EWSAA (P.L. 108-11) effectively restores immunity to Iraqi assets. While this argument has not prevailed in the courts, and Congress included in § 1083(c) of the FY2008 NDAA a provision approving of the courts' interpretation that EWSAA could not be invoked to such effect (§ 1083(c)(4)), there may be some plausibility to the argument that Congress, by permitting the President to waive the latter provision, has tacitly acquiesced to the President's interpretation of EWSAA. The D.C. Circuit did not consider whether a waiver of § 1083(c)(4) had any effect on EWSAA, concluding that its earlier decision in Acree would control in any event. Simon, slip op. at 9. The Supreme Court may take up the issue if it grants certiorari in Republic of Iraq v. Beaty (docket no. 07-1090).

[165] P.L. 110-181, § 1083(d)(4).

[166] Ministry of Defense and Support for the Armed Forces of the Islamic Republic of Iran, v. Cubic Defense Systems, 385 F.3d 1206 (9th Cir. 2004), rev'd and remanded sub nom. Ministry of Defense and Support for the Armed Forces of the Islamic Republic of Iran v. Elahi, 546 U.S. 450 (2006).
[167] Elahi v. Islamic Republic of Iran, 124 F. Supp. 2d 97 (D.D.C. 2000).
[168] Flatow chose to receive 100 percent of his compensatory damages from U.S. funds, but in return was required to relinquish "all rights to execute against or attach property that is at issue in claims against the United States before an international tribunal, that is the subject of awards rendered by such tribunal, or that is subject to section 1610(f)(1)(A) of title 28, United States Code." The court found that the award was covered by section 1610(f)(1)(A) because it is property regulated (although not blocked) by the Office of Foreign Assets control.
[169] 28 U.S.C. § 1611(b) exempts from the exception to immunity in § 1610 property that "is, or is intended to be, used in connection with a military activity and (A) is of a military character, or (B) is under the control of a military authority or defense agency." The contract dispute underlying the arbitral award had to do with non-delivery of defense equipment.
[170] 383 F.3d at 1222-23.
[171] Id. at 1223.
[172] 546 U.S. 450 (2006).
[173] 28 U.S.C. § 1610(a).
[174] 495 F.3d 1024 (9th Cir. 2007).
[175] Id. at 1033-35. See supra note 71 for definition of "blocked asset."
[176] Docket No. 07-615.
[177] See Brief of the Solicitor General in Support of Certiorari, Elahi v. Islamic Republic of Iran (U.S.)(No. 07-615).
[178] See H.Rept. 110-477 (to accompany H.R. 1585).
[179] See Notification of the Veto of H.R. 1585, supra note 151.
[180] Punitive damages are available under other exceptions to the FSIA only with respect to agencies and instrumentalities of foreign governments. The FSIA provision for liability and damages is 22 U.S.C. § 1606: As to any claim for relief with respect to which a foreign state is not entitled to immunity under section 1605 or 1607 of this chapter, the foreign state shall be liable in the same manner and to the same extent as a private individual under like circumstances; but a foreign state except for an agency or instrumentality thereof shall not be liable for punitive damages; if, however, in any case wherein death was caused, the law of the place where the action or omission occurred provides, or has been construed to provide, for

damages only punitive in nature, the foreign state shall be liable for actual or compensatory damages measured by the pecuniary injuries resulting from such death which were incurred by the persons for whose benefit the action was brought. The Flatow Amendment permitted punitive damages against "an official, employee, or agent of a foreign state." P.L. 104-208, Title I, §101(c) [Title V, § 589] (September 30, 1996), 110 Stat. 3009-172; codified at 28 U.S.C. § 1605 note. Some courts have awarded punitive damages against foreign governments and officials (including heads of State) by construing them to be agencies, instrumentalities, agents, employees, or officials or by reference to the doctrine of vicarious liability. See Appendix A for damages awarded in particular cases.

[181] Members of the Armed Services who are not U.S. citizens would likely be considered U.S. nationals. See, e.g., Peterson v. Islamic Republic of Iran, 515 F. Supp. 2d 25, 40 (D.D.C. 2007). Nothing in the FSIA expressly excludes servicemembers and their family members from suing under the terrorism exception, but some judges have applied a test to determine whether servicemembers are serving in a non-combatant role. See Estate of Heiser v. Islamic Republic of Iran, 466 F. Supp. 2d 229, 258 (D.D.C. 2006); Peterson v. Islamic Republic of Iran, 264 F. Supp. 2d 46 (D.D.C. 2003); Blais v. Islamic Republic of Iran, 459 F. Supp. 2d 40 (D.D.C. 2006); Prevatt v. Islamic Republic of Iran, 421 F. Supp. 2d 152 (D.D.C. 2006); Dammarell v. Islamic Republic of Iran, 404 F. Supp. 2d 261 (D.D.C. 2005); Salazar v. Islamic Republic of Iran, 370 F. Supp. 2d 105 (D.D.C. 2005).

[182] See supra at 27-32 (describing Roeder case).

[183] It appears the plaintiffs in the case have filed a new claim. Roeder v. Islamic Republic of Iran, Civil Case No. 1:2008cv00487 (D.D.C. filed March 21, 2008).

[184] 28 U.S.C. § 1605A(b). Prior to amendment, the FSIA specified that calculations of the statute of limitations in these cases are subject to equitable tolling, "including the period during which the foreign state was immune from suit." 28 U.S.C. § 1605(f). Some courts had interpreted the equitable tolling provision to extend the statute of limitations to 10 years beyond the enactment of the original § 1605(a)(7) in 1996, while other courts had not, which resulted in the dismissal of some claims filed prior to the new cut-off date in April 2006. However, the D.C. Circuit has found that the statute of limitations under the original § 1605(a)(7) was meant to extend to April 2006 for claims arising prior to April 1996. Simon v. Republic of Iraq, 2008 WL 2497417 (D.C. Cir. 2008), rev'g in part Vine v. Republic of Iraq, 459 F. Supp. 2d 10 (2006).

[185] 28 U.S.C. § 1605A(a)(2). The defendant State must also have been a designated sponsor of terrorism when the act occurred or subsequently designated as such as a result of the act of terrorism that gives rise to the claim, as long as it "remains so designated when the claim is filed" or "was so designated within the 6-month period before the claim is filed."

[186] Peterson v. Islamic Republic of Iran, 264 F. Supp. 2d 46 (D.D.C. 2003)(suit brought by those injured as a result of the 1983 bombing of the Marine barracks in Lebanon). Special masters were appointed in this case, which involved nearly one thousand plaintiffs, and damages of $2,656,944,877.00 were awarded. Peterson v. Islamic Republic of Iran, 515 F. Supp. 2d 25 (D.D.C. 2007). A default judgment was entered against Iran in another case involving the Marine barracks bombing, Valore v. Islamic Republic of Iran, 478 F. Supp. 2d 101 (D.D.C. 2007), and a special master has been assigned to determine damages.

[187] Prejudgment attachments of property used for commercial activity in the United States owned by a foreign government are permissible only if the foreign state expressly waives sovereign immunity for that purpose. 28 U.S.C. § 1610(d).

[188] "Tangible personal property" is not defined. Personal property is generally understood to encompass property that is not real property, that is, real estate. Tangible property is generally understood to mean "all property which is touchable and has real existence (physical) whether real or personal," while "intangible property" is "such property as has no intrinsic and marketable value, but is merely the representative or evidence of value." BLACK'S LAW DICTIONARY 809, 1217 (6th ed.1990). However, some courts have treated cash, stock certificates, and the like as tangible, at least in some contexts, while other courts treat currency and stock as intangible representations of value.

[189] "Controlled by" is not further defined. Under 28 U.S.C. § 1610, as amended, the property of a foreign State (including interests held directly or indirectly in a separate juridical entity), is subject to execution regardless of the level of economic control the State exercises over the property or the degree to which officials of that government manage the property or otherwise have a hand in its daily affairs. It may be questioned whether lobbyists or attorneys registered as agents of a State sponsor (or former sponsor) of terrorism under the Foreign Agents Registration Act (FARA), 22 U.S.C. §§ 611 et seq., are entities "controlled by" that for the purpose of 28 U.S.C. §§ 1605A(g) and 1610(g) such that their property would be subject to lis pendens.

[190] 28 U.S.C. § 1655. This provision is for the enforcement of an actual lien, which creates an enforceable property interest, so it would not likely apply to lis pendens notices.
[191] 28 U.S.C. § 1964 (constructive notice of pending action involving real estate).
[192] Most states require that (1) the complaint must raise the issue of interest in or title to real property; (2) the property affected must be sufficiently described; and (3) the notice must be filed with or after, but not prior to, the complaint.
[193] 54 C.J.S. Lis Pendens § 31 (1987).
[194] Id. § 11.
[195] Id. § 10.
[196] 51 AM. JUR. 2D Lis Pendens § 2.
[197] Id. § 34.
[198] 51 AM. JUR. 2D Lis Pendens § 51.
[199] Id. § 65.
[200] 54 C.J.S. Lis Pendens § 34.
[201] The requirement that the property be subject to attachment under 28 U.S.C. § 1610 can be read two ways. It can be read to require that the property would be subject to execution to satisfy a judgment based on the specific claim at issue because it is property described in 28 U.S.C. § 1610(g), or it can be read to require merely that the property does not qualify for foreign sovereign immunity. The legislative history suggests that the intent is to protect property used for diplomatic or consular purposes rather than to ensure that lis pendens notices have effect only with respect to property that is ultimately subject to attachment to satisfy a judgment on a particular claim. This interpretation is problematic because the provision seems to cover all property titled in any entity identified by the plaintiff as controlled by the defendant state, which could encompass property in which the defendant state has no interest, and where the property owner is not a defendant to the action.
[202] 28 U.S.C. § 1964.
[203] 54 C.J.S. Lis Pendens § 23.
[204] Id. § 24.
[205] See Connecticut v. Doehr, 501 U.S. 1, 11 (1991) (prejudgment measures affecting property rights, even if short of property seizure, must comport with due process). However, numerous courts have validated state lis pendens statutes providing for constructive notice if recordation procedures

were followed, even without prior notice and a hearing for the property owner. See 51 AM. JUR. 2D Lis Pendens § 9.

[206] At least seven such suits have yielded default judgments. In Martinez v. Republic of Cuba, No. 99-018208 CA 1 (Miami-Dade Co., Fla., 11th Cir. Ct. decided March 9, 2001), a woman was awarded $27.1 million by the Miami-Dade Court, Florida, for sexual battery based on her marriage by fraud to a Cuban spy. In Weininger v. Republic of Cuba, No. 03-22920 CA 20 (Miami-Dade Co., Fla., 11th Cir. Ct. decided November 11, 2004), the same court awarded $86,562,000.00 to the daughter of a CIA pilot who was shot down over Cuba during the Bay of Pigs invasion and subsequently executed. The court also awarded $67 million to the daughter of a U.S. businessman who was tried as a spy and executed in the aftermath of the Cuban Revolution, McCarthy v. Republic of Cuba, No. 01-28628 CA04 (Miami-Dade Co., Fla., 11th Cir. Ct. decided April 17, 2003), and $400 million to the siblings and daughter of a plantation owner's son executed after by the Castro regime a sham military trial, Hausler v. Republic of Cuba, No. 02-12475 CA 01 (Miami-Dade Co., Fla., 11th Cir. Ct., decided January 19, 2007). In Jerez v. Republic of Cuba, No. 05-18719 CA 9 (Miami-Dade Co., Fla., 11th Cir. Ct., decided January 30, 2007), the court awarded $200 million to a Cuban dissident arrested in 1964 and thereafter subjected to torture in prison and in a psychiatric hospital. (Jerez does not involve a U.S. citizen and does not appear to rely on the FSIA for jurisdiction, leaving the jurisdictional basis unclear). In Vera v. Republic of Cuba, No. 01-31216-CA-01 (Miami-Dade Co., Fla., 11th Cir. Ct., decided May 15, 2008), the court awarded $94.6 million to the estate and family of a dissident who was murdered in Puerto Rico in 1976, and in Suarez v. Republic of Cuba, No. 05-25387 CA-27 (Miami-Dade Co., Fla., 11th Cir. Ct., decided April 4, 2008), the court awarded $253 million to the family of a former friend of Fidel Castro who was imprisoned in 1959 and died in prison in 1977. (Cuba was designated a state sponsor of terrorism in 1982).

[207] In vetoing the original bill, President Bush argued that the provision would permit plaintiffs to obtain liens on certain Iraqi property simply by filing a notice of pending action. Liens under section 1083 would be automatic upon filing a notice of a pending claim in a judicial district where Iraq's property is located, and they would reach property up to the amount of the judgment plaintiffs choose to demand in their complaints. Such pre-judgment liens, entered before claims are tested and cases are heard, are extraordinary and have never previously been available in suits in U.S. courts against foreign sovereigns. If permitted to become law, even for a

short time, section 1083's attachment and lien provisions would impose grave — indeed, intolerable — consequences on Iraq. Notification of the Veto of H.R. 1585, supra note 151. Businesses could also be deterred by the lis pendens and other assets provisions of § 1083 from engaging in commercial transactions with Libya. See Sue Pleming, U.S. Ties with Libya Strained over New Law, REUTERS (February 22, 2008) (noting criticism by Libyan diplomats and the U.S.-Libya Business Association, who argues the law will threaten trade by raising "major litigation risks" for U.S. businesses seeking to take advantage of renewed ties with Libya).

[208] In order for property to be attached, it must also fall under an exception to sovereign immunity or otherwise fail to qualify for immunity. 28 U.S.C. § 1610(a)(7) abrogates immunity with respect to the property of a foreign State used for a commercial activity in the United States when "the judgment relates to a claim for which the foreign state is not immune" under section 1605A or predecessor statute, "regardless of whether the property is or was involved with the act upon which the claim is based." (This exception does not apply to foreign central bank or monetary authority held for its own account or property of a military character or that belongs to a military authority. 28 U.S.C. § 1611(b)). Any property belonging to an agency or instrumentality of a foreign State engaged in commercial activity in the United States is not immune from attachment to satisfy judgments under section 1605A, regardless of whether the property is used for commercial activity or relates to the claim..

[209] This clause appears designed to avoid the application of the Supreme Court decision in First Nat'l City Bank v. Banco Para El Comercio Exterior de Cuba, 462 U.S. 611 (1983) ("Bancec") to judgments against designated terrorist States. Bancec held that duly-created instrumentalities of a foreign State are to be accorded a presumption of independent status, but that this presumption may be overcome where such recognition would permit the foreign State to pursue a claim in United States courts while itself escaping liability by asserting immunity. The proposed language could allow a judgment creditor to "pierce the corporate veil"of a corporation owned, in whole or in part, by a judgment debtor State without having to demonstrate to the court that the presumption of independent status should be overridden.

[210] See Peterson v. Islamic Republic of Iran, slip op., Civil Action No. 01-2094 (D.D.C. 2008) (order denying motion to appoint receivership to levy against bank holdings in foreign state-owned banks).

[211] H.Rept. 110-477, Conference Report to Accompany H.R. 1585, National Defense Authorization Act for Fiscal Year 2008, at 1001.
[212] See Flatow v. Islamic Republic of Iran, 67 F. Supp. 2d 535, 539 (D. Md. 1999), aff'd sub nom. Flatow v. Alavi Foundation, 225 F.3d 653 (4th Cir. 2000) (holding "a principal-agent relationship has been created for the purposes of the FSIA when the foreign sovereign exercises day-to-day control over its activities"(citing McKesson Corp. v. Islamic Republic of Iran, 52 F.3d 346, 351-52 (D.C. Cir.1995); see also Hester Int'l Corp. v. Federal Republic of Nigeria, 879 F.2d 170, 178-80 (5th Cir.1989) (holding that an entity in which Nigeria held 100% of its stock was not an agent because there was no showing of day-to-day control); Baglab Ltd. v. Johnson Matthey Bankers Ltd., 665 F. Supp. 289, 297 (S.D.N.Y. 1987) (holding that the plaintiff failed to overcome the presumption of separateness because it failed to prove that the Bank of England exercised "general control over the day-to-day activities" of an entity so that the entity could be deemed an agent).
[213] See Alejandre v. Telefonico Larga Distancia de Puerto Rico, 183 F.3d 1277, 1283 and n. 13 (11th Cir. 1999) (noting the court "conduct[s] exactly the same inquiry in order to determine both whether an exception to the Cuban Government's immunity from garnishment also applies to [Empresa de Telecomunicaciones de Cuba, S.A. ("ETECSA")] and whether ETECSA can be held substantively liable for the Government's debt to the plaintiffs: namely, whether the plaintiffs have overcome the presumption that ETECSA is a juridical entity separate from the Government"). But see Dole Food Co. v. Patrickson, 538 U.S. 468, 477 (2003) (foreign government's control over day-to-day operations of subsidiary company was not relevant to establishing whether the company was itself an "instrumentality" of that government for purposes of immunity; the direct ownership of a majority of shares was the controlling factor).
[214] See Flatow, 67 F. Supp. 2d at 538 ("In order to levy against a third-party's property, the judgment creditor must prove that the property of a third-party can be seized because: (1) the third-party is an agent, alter ego, or instrumentality of the judgment debtor; (2) the third-party is a garnishee of the judgment debtor; or (3) there was a conveyance of property between the judgment debtor and the third-party which was motivated by the intent to defrauding creditors."). In this case, the third-party owner of the property was found not to be an agency or instrumentality of a foreign government because it was a corporation formed under the laws of New York.

[215] The provision could be construed as intended to overturn results in cases like Flatow v. Alavi Foundation, 225 F.3d 653 (4th Cir. 2000), in which a judgment creditor made an unsuccessful effort to levy against real property owned by a corporation that was neither an agency or instrumentality of Iran nor a subsidiary of such an agency or instrumentality, and the Bancec test was not found to be met. It is unclear how the removal of the Bancec test for determining third-party liability will assist the court in determining the sovereign ownership of a property interest that a creditor seeks to attach, without the use of a separate test for determining ownership, which § 1083 does not provide.

[216] For a corporation to qualify as an agency or instrumentality of a foreign government, the foreign government must own directly a majority of its shares. Dole Food Co. v. Patrickson, 538 U.S. 468 (2003). Subsidiary companies owned by an instrumentality of a foreign government are not themselves instrumentalities of the foreign government.

[217] H.Rept. 110-477 at 1001-02.

[218] Id.

[219] Cf. Weininger v. Castro, 462 F. Supp. 2d 457, 485 (S.D.N.Y. 2006) (interpreting TRIA § 201, which makes subject to levy "the blocked assets of [the defendant] terrorist party (including the blocked assets of any agency or instrumentality of that terrorist party)" to "obviate analysis of the Bancec presumption"). Like TRIA § 201, new 28 U.S.C. § 2610(g) permits the use of the assets of an agency or instrumentality of a State sponsor of terrorism to be used to satisfy terrorism judgments against the State itself. Compare 28 U.S.C. § 2610(g) with § 2610(f)(1), which provides that blocked and regulated property is "subject to execution or attachment in aid of execution of any judgment relating to a claim for which a foreign state (including any agency or instrumentality of such state) claiming such property is not immune [under the terrorism exception]." This provision has been interpreted as not obviating the Bancec presumption. 462 F. Supp. 2d at 486 (citing Alejandre v. Telefonica Larga Distancia de Puerto Rico, Inc., 183 F.3d 1277, 1287 (11th Cir.1999)).

[220] For a court to recognize a waiver of U.S. sovereign immunity, it must be "unequivocally expressed in the statutory text" and "is to be strictly construed, in terms of its scope, in favor of the sovereign." See Weinstein at 56 (citing Department of the Army v. Blue Fox, Inc., 525 U.S. 255, 261 (1999)).

[221] See, e.g., 31 C.F.R.§ 335.203(e) ("Unless licensed or authorized pursuant to this part any attachment, judgment, decree, lien, execution, garnishment, or

other judicial process is null and void with respect to any property in which on or since the effective date there existed an interest of Iran."); 31 C.F.R. § 575.203(e) (same, with respect to Iraq).

[222] TRIA § 201(d)(2) defines 'blocked asset' to mean property seized or frozen pursuant to certain sanctions, but not property that may be transferred pursuant to a license that is required by statute other than IEEPA or the United Nations Participation Act of 1945. It also excludes diplomatic or consular property being used solely for diplomatic or consular purposes, from the definition of "blocked asset." TRIA does not refer to regulated assets, so it is unclear whether "blocked" and "regulated" are mutually exclusive terms, or whether "blocked" assets would be considered to be "regulated" as well. At least one court has found that the two terms are not equivalent. See Weinstein v. Islamic Republic of Iran, 299 F. Supp. 2d 63, 76 (E.D.N.Y. 2004) (rejecting the argument that TRIA equates "regulated" with "blocked"). In any event, TRIA § 201 remains in force for use in efforts to attach blocked property to satisfy judgments that were awarded under 28 U.S.C. § 1605(a)(7), subject to the applicable restrictions, apparently even if the property would otherwise be immune under 28 U.S.C. §§ 1610 or 1611.

[223] See Flatow v. Islamic Republic of Iran, 74 F. Supp. 2d 18 (D.D.C. 1999) (holding that FSIA terrorist State provisions exceptions did not authorize attachment of United States Treasury funds owed to Iran in accordance with an award of the Iran-United States Claims Tribunal, as such funds remained the property of the United States, and the amendments did not contain the express and unequivocal waiver required to abrogate the United States' sovereign immunity).

[224] See Weinstein, 299 F. Supp. 2d at 58 ("[F]unds held in the U.S. Treasury — even though set aside or 'earmarked' for a specific purpose — remain the property of the United States until the government elects to pay them to whom they are owed."). For more information about the FMS account and its contents, see supra notes 50-51.

[225] 225 Fed. R. Civ. Pro. 60(b) provides On motion and upon such terms as are just, the court may relieve a party or a party's legal representative from a final judgment, order, or proceeding for the following reasons: (1) mistake, inadvertence, surprise, or excusable neglect; (2) newly discovered evidence which by due diligence could not have been discovered in time to move for a new trial under Rule 59 (b); (3) fraud (whether heretofore denominated intrinsic or extrinsic), misrepresentation, or other misconduct of an adverse party; (4) the judgment is void; (5) the judgment has been satisfied,

released, or discharged, or a prior judgment upon which it is based has been reversed or otherwise vacated, or it is no longer equitable that the judgment should have prospective application; or (6) any other reason justifying relief from the operation of the judgment. The motion shall be made within a reasonable time, and for reasons (1), (2), and (3) not more than one year after the judgment, order, or proceeding was entered or taken. A motion under this subdivision (b) does not affect the finality of a judgment or suspend its operation. This rule does not limit the power of a court to entertain an independent action to relieve a party from a judgment, order, or proceeding, or to grant relief to a defendant not actually personally notified as provided in Title 28, U.S.C., § 1655, or to set aside a judgment for fraud upon the court. Writs of coram nobis, coram vobis, audita querela, and bills of review and bills in the nature of a bill of review, are abolished, and the procedure for obtaining any relief from a judgment shall be by motion as prescribed in these rules or by an independent action.

[226] In some cases, federal statute may provide a cause of action. See Rux v. Republic of Sudan, 495 F. Supp. 2d 541 (E.D. Va. 2007) (Death on the High Seas Act, 41 Stat. 537, 46 U.S.C. app. §§ 761-67, applied to suit involving the terrorist attack on the U.S.S. Cole in 2000).

[227] Several efforts to reopen cases to assess punitive damages have been rebuffed by the courts on the basis that the plaintiffs had not filed a motion for relief from judgment on or prior to January 28, 2008. E.g. Steen v. Iran, Slip Copy, 2008 WL 1800778 (D.D.C. April 21, 2008) (request for additional damages); Higgins v. Iran, Slip Copy, 2008 WL 1787720 (D.D.C. April 21, 2008) (effort to add punitive damages to award against Iran that already includes $300 million in punitive damages against the Iranian Islamic Revolutionary Guard Corps); Holland v. Iran, Slip Copy, 2008 WL 1787721 (D.D.C. April 21, 2008). The court rejected all these plaintiffs' contention that their right to pursue execution of their judgments kept their cases "open before the courts in any form...as of [January 28, 2008]" within the meaning of § 1083(c).

[228] Plaintiffs who already have a judgment against Iran for $317 million ($300 million of which is punitive damages against Ayatollah Khamanei personally, and none of which has been satisfied), Bodoff v. Islamic Republic of Iran, 424 F. Supp. 2d 74 (D.D.C. 2006), have filed a new action against Iran, the Ayatollah Khamanei, and other defendants pursuant to new § 1605A. Bodoff v. Islamic Republic of Iran, Case No. 1:2008cv00547 (D.D.C. filed March 18, 2008). See also Rubin v. Islamic Republic of Iran, Case No. 1:2008cv00521 (D.D.C. filed March 26, 2008) (plaintiffs who

have judgments amounting to nearly $110 million, nearly all of which remains uncollected, filed action against Iran and its Ministry of Information Security and several officials for the same suicide bombing in Jerusalem that gave rise to their original judgments); Ben Haim v. Islamic Republic of Iran, Case No. 1:2008cv00520 (D.D.C. filed March 26, 2008); Goldberg-Botvin v. Islamic Republic of Iran, Case No. 1:2008cv00503 (D.D.C. filed March 24, 2008).

[229] P.L. 110-181 §1083(c)(3). It is unclear whether the "original lawsuit" is restricted to the first lawsuit filed based on a specific act of terrorism or whether any currently or previously pending lawsuit based on the same incident will suffice. It is also unclear whether claims that were dismissed prior to the enactment of P.L. 110-181 for reasons other than (or in addition to) a finding that the Flatow Amendment (28 U.S.C. § 1605 note) or 28 U.S.C. § 1605(a)(7) (as previously in effect) did not create a cause of action against the State (as required for refiling a "pending" but finally adjudicated claim under §1083(c)(2)) will succeed in bringing the claim anew as an action related to another lawsuit under §1083(c)(3). For example, one case involving a terrorist hijacking that took place in 1985 was dismissed as time-barred in 2007. Estate of Buonocore v. Libya, 2007 WL 2007509 (D.D.C. 2007)(dismissing all claims with prejudice because plaintiffs had not filed within reasonable time after enactment of terrorist state exception to the FSIA in April 1996). Plaintiffs have brought a new lawsuit based on the same facts, Simpson v. Libya, Case No. 1:2008cv00529 (D.D.C. filed March 27, 2008). If this lawsuit is construed to be a "refilled action" within the meaning of § 1083(c)(2)(B)(ii), then Libya would be disabled from contesting the suit based on the expiration of the statute of limitations.

[230] See Landgraf v. USI Film Products, 511 U.S. 244, 273-280 (1994); United States v. Schooner Peggy, 5 U.S. (1 Cranch) 103, 110 (1801).

[231] See Plaut v. Spendthrift Farms, 514 U.S. 211 (1995) (invalidating statute that required federal courts to reopen certain suits related to securities fraud that were dismissed as time barred after the Supreme Court had interpreted a previous statute to establish uniform limitations period for such cases).

[232] See, e.g., id. at 230 ("Congress has the power to waive the res judicata effect of a prior judgment entered in the Government's favor on a claim against the United States." (citing United States v. Sioux Nation, 448 U.S. 371, 397 (1980))); Cherokee Nation v. United States, 270 U.S. 476 (1926); United States v. Central Eureka Mining Company, 357 U.S. 155, 174-177 (1958) (Frankfurter, J., dissenting) (citing legislation in which Congress has

waived legal defense in conjunction with waiving U.S. sovereign immunity).

[233] See supra at 33-35 (discussing waiver authority with respect to actions against Iraq).

[234] See supra at 40-41.

[235] For more information about legislation regarding Libya's terrorist acts, see CRS Report RL33142, Libya: Background and U.S. Relations, by Christopher M. Blanchard.

[236] 28 U.S.C. § 1605A(a)(2).

[237] See supra note 229. It is not clear whether a settlement constitutes a "judgment" for this purpose.

[238] See U.S.-Libya Business Association, Current and Potential Trade and Investment Opportunities in Libya, January 11, 2008 (arguing that potential property attachments are harmful to U.S. parties with existing contracts and discourage parties from considering future export possibilities).

[239] Correspondence from the U.S.-Libya Business Association, the National Foreign Trade Council, the National Association of Manufacturers, and the United States Chamber of Commerce to U.S. Secretary of State Condoleezza Rice, February 28, 2008 (urging the Administration to seek waiver authority with respect to Libya).

[240] Text of the Administration proposal was included in the correspondence from U.S.-Secretary of State Condoleezza Rice, U.S. Secretary of Defense Robert Gates, U.S. Secretary of Energy Samuel Bodman, and U.S. Secretary of Commerce Carlos Gutierrez to Speaker of the House Nancy Pelosi, Senate Majority Leaders Harry Reid, et al., March 18, 2008.

[241] See Appendix A.

[242] Press Release, U.S. Department of State, Joint Statement by the United States and Libya, May 30, 2008, available at [http://www.state.gov/r/pa/prs/ps/2008/may/105466.htm].

[243] See Arshad Mohammed, U.S., Libya near Deal to Compensate Terror Victims, REUTERS (July 31, 2008), available at [http://in.reuters.com/article/worldNews/idINIndia-34755220080731] (describing tentative agreement between United States and Libya that "hinges on action by the U.S. Congress" to provide compensation possibly worth as much as $1 billion to victims of terrorism for which Libya has been blamed).

[244] 31 U.S.C. §§ 9101 - 9110. For information about such corporations, see CRS Report RL30365, Federal Government Corporations: An Overview, by Kevin R. Kosar.

[245] 28 U.S.C. § 1605A provides a cause of action for "personal injury or death," which appears to cover a broader scope of injuries than "wrongful death or physical injury." Claims for wrongful death under the FSIA amendment have been limited to the decedent's estate, while close relatives of a victim have recovered in their own right based on claims of solatium, intentional infliction of emotional distress, and pain and suffering, depending on the applicable state law. See, e.g., Pugh v. Libya, 530 F. Supp. 2d 216 (D.D.C. 2008).

[246] Price v. Libya, 384 F. Supp. 2d 120 (D.D.C. 2005)(approximately $18 million judgment against Libya for injuries suffered during plaintiffs' imprisonment pending trial for allegedly taking unlawful photographs); Pugh v. Libya, 530 F. Supp. 2d 216 (D.D.C. 2008)(nearly $7 billion judgment against Libya and six named officials for bombing of a French airliner over Africa in 1989).

[247] Sec. 1(a)(3) (including case 1:00CV00716 in the U.S. District Court for the District of Columbia). It appears that these plaintiffs would also be eligible under § 1(a)(1), since they have obtained a judgment against Iran that has not yet been fully satisfied. The plaintiffs received partial compensation pursuant to § 2002 of the Victims of Trafficking Act. See Appendix A.

[248] Press Release, U.S. Department of State, Rescission of Libya's Designation as a State Sponsor of Terrorism, March 15, 2006, available at [http://www.state.gov/r/pa/prs/ps/2006/66244.htm].

[249] Law Library of Congress, Suits Against Terrorist States: Cuba (February 2002) (Rept. No. 2002-11904).

[250] Law Library of Congress, Iran: Suits Against Americans for Acts of Terrorism (July 2003) (Rept. No. 2003-14887).

[251] See Michael Theodoulou, Tehran Court Rules Against US, CHRISTIAN SCIENCE MONITOR, February 3, 2003, at 6.

[252] See Michael Theodoulou, US Embassy is Seized Again to Settle Pounds 270m 'Compensation' Order, TIMES (U.K.), April 13, 2007, at 44. An Iranian official reportedly denied that the U.S. embassy had been seized, noting that such a judicial sale of embassy property would violate the Vienna Convention on Diplomatic Relations. US Embassy Auction Rejected, IRAN DAILY (April 17, 2007); Iran Says Us Embassy Not for Sale, KHALEEJ TIMES ONLINE (April 16, 2007).

[253] See Julie Kay, Miami Lawyers Race Each Other to Frozen Cuban Funds, MIAMI DAILY BUS. REV., October 1, 2007, at 1 (reporting difficulties judgment creditors of Cuba experience in recovering damages). According to the Calendar Year 2006 Fifteenth Annual Report to the Congress on

Assets in the United States of Terrorist Countries and International Terrorism Program Designees (September 2007), prepared by the Office of Foreign Assets Control, the nearly $200 million of assets blocked under the Cuban sanctions regulations includes blocked assets of all Cuban nationals such as blocked wire transfers intended for or sent by Cuban nationals, as well as "assets owned by third parties that have been blocked due to the indirect or contingent interest of the Cuban government or Cuban nationals." Id. at 9-10.

In: Suits Against Terrorist...
Editor: Beatrice V. Mohoney

ISBN 978-1-60692-835-6
© 2009 Nova Science Publishers, Inc.

Chapter 2

LAWSUITS AGAINST STATE SUPPORTERS OF TERRORISM: AN OVERVIEW*

Jennifer K. Elsea

ABSTRACT

> A 1996 amendment to the Foreign Sovereign Immunities Act (FSIA) enables American victims of international terrorist acts supported by certain States designated by the State Department as sponsors of terrorism — Cuba, Iran, North Korea, Sudan, Syria, and previously Iraq and Libya — to bring suit in U.S. courts for damages. Despite congressional efforts to make blocked (or "frozen") assets of such States available for attachment by judgment creditors in such cases, plaintiffs encountered difficulties in enforcing the awards. Congress passed, as part of the National Defense Authorization Act for FY2008 (NDAA) (H.R. 1585), an amendment to the FSIA to provide a federal cause of action against terrorist States and to facilitate enforcement of judgments. After the President vetoed the NDAA based on the possible impact the measure would have on Iraqi assets, Congress passed a new version, P.L. 110-181 (H.R. 4986), which includes authority for the President to waive the FSIA provision with respect to Iraq. Congress later passed a measure to exempt Libya if it agrees to compensate victims (S. 3370).

---

* Excerpted from CRS Report RS22094, dated August 7, 2008.

In 1996, Congress amended the FSIA to allow civil suits by U.S. victims of terrorism against designated State sponsors of terrorism (DSST) [1] responsible for, or complicit in, such terrorist acts as torture, extrajudicial killing, aircraft sabotage, and hostage taking. 28 U.S.C. § 1605(a)(7). Congress also abrogated the immunity of foreign State assets under the FSIA to satisfy judgments awarded under the terrorism exception. 28 U.S.C. § 1610. After a court found that the abrogation of sovereign immunity did not itself create a cause of action, Congress passed the "Flatow Amendment," 28 U.S.C. § 1605 note, to create a cause of action for such cases. Courts initially interpreted the statute as creating a cause of action against foreign States and their agencies and instrumentalities, although its plain language referred only to officials, employees, and agents of such States. Numerous court judgments, generally rendered after the defendants' default, ensued, resulting in substantial awards to plaintiffs.

The nature of lawsuits against DSSTs changed significantly after the D.C. Circuit Court of Appeals held that neither the terrorism exception to the FSIA nor the Flatow Amendment created a private right of action against the foreign government itself, including its agencies and instrumentalities. Consequently, most plaintiffs asserted causes of action under domestic state laws, which resulted in some disparity in the relief available to victims injured due to similar or even the same acts of terrorism. Courts nevertheless continued to award sizable judgments against DSSTs and their officials, which now amount to more than $18 billion in damages, most of which has been assessed against Iran. See CRS Report RL3 1258, Suits Against Terrorist States by Victims of Terrorism, by Jennifer K. Elsea.

ENFORCEMENT OF JUDGMENTS AGAINST TERRORIST STATES

While winning judgments against terrorist States never posed insurmountable obstacles, enforcing those judgments has proven more arduous, primarily due to the scarcity of assets within U.S. jurisdiction that belong to States subject to economic sanctions and the immunity from attachment that assets frozen by sanctions regulations enjoy. Successive Administrations opposed allowing the use of frozen assets of foreign States to satisfy judgments out of concerns for treaty obligations to protect foreign diplomatic and consular properties, the desire to maintain the blocked assets for diplomatic leverage, and the concern that permitting the attachment of such assets would expose U.S. assets abroad to reciprocal action. Notwithstanding these objections, Congress has repeatedly stepped in to make more foreign assets available for judgment creditors, and appropriated some $400 million to pay portions of certain judgments against Iran with the understanding that the President would seek to recover that amount from Iran. Consequently, some plaintiffs were able to collect portions of their judgments, while others were stymied. Some of the assets associated with DSSTs remained off-limits because they were not "blocked" within the meaning of the relevant statute; because plaintiffs had waived their right to attach the assets in question when they accepted payment from U.S. funds; because the assets were not subject to the exception to immunity or were exempted by presidential waiver; or because the United States validly possesses the property and successfully asserted U.S. sovereign immunity.

THE NATIONAL DEFENSE AUTHORIZATION ACT FOR FY2008

In order to assist plaintiffs, Congress passed § 1083 of the National Defense Authorization Act for FY2008 (NDAA) (P.L. 110-181), to create § 1 605A in title 28, U.S. Code. Section 1083 incorporates the terrorist State exception to the FSIA previously codified at 28 U.S.C. § 1605(a)(7), and a new cause of action against DSSTs to replace the Flatow Amendment. It allows U.S. nationals (and non-U.S. nationals working for the U.S. government overseas) who are harmed by terrorism to seek compensatory as well as punitive damages (which are not otherwise available against foreign States). The provision also seeks to make more assets associated with State sponsors of terrorism available for attachment in aid of execution of terrorism judgments, and to permit some plaintiffs to refile claims.

President Bush vetoed the original version of the NDAA, H.R. 1585, on the stated basis that the FSIA amendments would threaten Iraq's economic security. Congress responded with the new version, H.R. 4986, which authorizes the President to waive any provision of § 1083 with respect to Iraq. The President signed the bill and exercised the waiver authority. Section 1083 also encourages the President to negotiate a settlement of outstanding terrorism claims against Iraq. Pending cases have been permitted to go forward under the previous law, but it is unclear whether any Iraqi assets will remain available for attachment by judgment holders under other provisions of law.

New 28 U.S.C. § 1605A(g) provides for the establishment of a lien of lis pendens with respect to all real or tangible personal property within the judicial district that is subject to attachment in aid of execution and is titled in the name of a defendant State or any entities listed by the plaintiff as "controlled by" that State. Ordinarily, lis pendens in civil litigation is used to put third parties on notice that the property is the subject of litigation, which effectively prevents the alienation of such property, although the notice is not technically a lien. Under the new provision, the clerk of the district court is required to file the notice of action indexed by listing the defendant and its controlled entities. This may relieve plaintiffs of the burden of identifying specific property in the notices, but it is unclear what further measures might be required to ensure adequate notice is afforded to prospective purchasers under the procedure or how it is to be determined without further process that the property is in fact subject to attachment. In the case of State sponsors of terror, whose property for the most part is already subject to substantial limitations on transactions, the primary utility may be the establishment of a line of priority among lien-holders. However, in the case of States that are no longer subject to terrorism sanctions, such as Libya, the provision could have some impact on lawful transactions.

New 28 U.S.C. § 16 10(g) provides that the property of a foreign State against which a judgment has been entered under §1605A (or predecessor provision), or of an agency or instrumentality of such a foreign State, "including property that is a separate juridical entity or is an interest held directly or indirectly in a separate juridical entity," is subject to attachment in aid of execution and execution upon that judgment, regardless of how much economic control over that property the foreign government exercises and whether the government derives profits or benefits from it. The President has no waiver authority (except with respect to Iraq). The provision may enable a plaintiff to "pierce the corporate veil"of a corporation owned, in whole or in part, by a judgment debtor State without having to demonstrate to the court that the presumption of independent status should be overridden. It could also be read as an effort to make any entity in which the defendant State (including its separate agencies and instrumentalities) has any interest liable for the terrorism-related judgments awarded against that State. On the other hand, § 16 10(g) states that nothing in it is to be construed as superceding the court's authority to protect the interests of a person "who is not liable in the action giving rise to a judgment."

Section 1610(g) also makes a property that is regulated by reason of U.S. sanctions available to satisfy terrorism judgments. It does not explicitly waive U.S. sovereign immunity, but appears designed to defeat provisions in the sanctions regulations that make blocked property effectively immune from court action. In this respect, it echoes language in § 1610(f)(1) (which is not in effect because it was waived by President Clinton), except that § 1610(g) applies only to regulated property rather than property that is blocked or regulated pursuant to sanctions regimes, [2] and it would not be subject to the presidential waiver in § 1620(f)(3). Unlike § 201 of TRIA (28 U.S.C. § 1610 note), the new language applies to regulated rather than blocked assets and it allows assets to be attached in aid of enforcing punitive damages.

The new provisions apply to any claim arising under them as well as to any action brought under former 28 U.S.C. § 1605(a)(7) or the Flatow Amendment that "relied on either of these provisions as creating a cause of action" and that "has been adversely affected on the grounds that either or both of these provisions fail to create a cause of action against the state," and that is still before the courts "in any form," including appeal or motion for post-judgment relief. In cases brought under the older provisions, the federal court in which the claim originated is required, on motion by the plaintiffs within 60 days after enactment, to treat the case as if it had been brought under the new provisions, apparently to include reinstating a vacated judgment. The measure waives a defendant's "defenses of res judicata, collateral estoppel and limitation period" in any reinstated action. The provision also permits the filing of new cases involving incidents that are already the subject of a timely-filed terrorism action under the FSIA, notwithstanding the limitation time for filing, so long as the related action is filed within 60 days after enactment (January 28, 2008) or entry of judgment in the original action. Several actions have been filed under this provision, including some lawsuits by plaintiffs who have already won significant judgments under the previous law.

While § 1083(c) refers to "pending cases," it appears to cover finally adjudicated cases in which litigants have filed a motion for relief from final judgment after appeals are exhausted. To the extent the provision is read to require courts to reopen final judgments or reinstate vacated judgments, it may be vulnerable to invalidation as an improper exercise of judicial powers by Congress. [3] A similar objection may be raised regarding the waiver of legal defenses: while it seems well-established that Congress can waive defenses in actions against the United States, an effort to abrogate legal defenses of other parties could raise constitutional due process and separation of powers issues. It may be that no cases qualify for reopening under this provision because the plaintiffs would have had to have filed a motion prior to the enactment of P.L. 110-181. However, if previous lawsuits can be filed again as "related actions" under § 1 083(c)(3), then plaintiffs who file prior to the deadline can bring new actions regardless of the reason their original case was unsuccessful or perhaps even if their case yielded an award. It is unclear whether such lawsuits would count as "refiled actions" for the purpose of abrogating the defendant's legal defenses under § 1803(c)(2)(B).

The new federal cause of action may make judgments against DSSTs heftier and easier to obtain, but whether such judgments will be easier to enforce seems less certain. The result may be an increase in debts owed by those States without a sufficient increase in assets available to cover them, which could amplify competition among plaintiffs and lead to calls for further congressional action. Transactions with debtor States are likely to increase only with respect to States that are no longer subject to anti-terrorism sanctions, in which case the use of their assets to satisfy judgments may act as a barrier to trade despite the lifting of sanctions. The presidential waiver for Iraq permits the President to protect Iraqi assets from attachment to satisfy any outstanding judgments. H.R. 5167 has been introduced in the House to repeal the presidential waiver provision.

EFFECT OF THE WAIVER OF § 1083 ON CASES PENDING AGAINST IRAQ

Section 1083(d) authorizes the President to waive any provision of §1083 with respect to Iraq if he determines that a waiver serves U.S. national security interests and promotes U.S.-Iraq relations, the waiver will promote reconstruction and political development in Iraq, and Iraq continues to be a reliable ally and partner in combating terrorism. The waiver applies retroactively regardless of its effect on pending cases.

On the day the President signed the FY2008 NDAA into law, the White House signed a waiver, [4] apparently foreclosing any refiling of the lawsuit by former prisoners of war against Iraq and Saddam Hussein for their mistreatment during the first Gulf War. [5] However, pending claims against Iraq under the FSIA terrorism exception (as previously in force) have been permitted to go forward. [6] Final judgments against Iraq are not affected, but will remain difficult to enforce. Iraqi government assets used for commercial purposes in the United States that are not subject to the protection of E.O. 13303, which covers the Development Fund for Iraq and all interests associated with Iraqi petroleum and petroleum products, may be subject to attachment and execution on terrorism judgments against Iraq under 28 U.S.C. § 1610. The President could, however, issue another executive order to protect all Iraqi assets from attachment to satisfy judgments.

ADMINISTRATION PROPOSAL TO WAIVE § 1083 FOR LIBYA

U.S. businesses seeking to establish a commercial relationship with Libya expressed concern that § 1083 will harm U.S.-Libya trade. [7] The Bush Administration, which has touted renewed U.S. investment in Libya and growth in bilateral trade as beneficial to the U.S. economy and as important tools for reestablishing relations with a reformed state sponsor of terrorism, appears to share their view.

To relieve Libya from the possible effects of § 1083 in the event Libya agrees to compensate victims of terrorism, Congress enacted S. 3370, the "Libyan Claims Resolution Act." S. 3370 exempts Libya from the terrorism exception to the FSIA if Libya signs a claims agreement with the United States to settle terrorism-related claims and provides funds to compensate claimants. S. 3370 authorizes the Secretary of State to designate one or more "entities" to assist in the provision of compensation. Entities would be immune from lawsuits related to this function. It appears that the government is to receive funds from Libya, which it would then turn over to the designated entity for dispersal to claimants, although there is no express requirement to this effect in the statute.

If the Secretary of State certifies to Congress that sufficient funds have been received under the claims agreement to cover settlements Libya has agreed to pay to victims of the Pan Am 103 airliner bombing and the La Belle Disco bombing, as well as to provide "fair compensation" to some other U.S. nationals who have pending cases against Libya, the statute will provide immunity to Libya, including its agencies and instrumentalities, as well as its officials, employees, and agents, for all claims pending under the terrorism exception to the FSIA, and for all property sought to be attached to satisfy existing terrorism judgments. It appears that the amount of fair compensation is left to the discretion of the Secretary of State. The provision may not include all pending cases against Libya under § 1605A. It appears to cover claims for wrongful death or physical injury arising under 28 U.S.C. § 1605A (including previous actions that have been given effect as if they had been filed under § 1605A), but not cases for non-physical injuries [8] or for cases filed under the previous version of the FSIA exception that have not been given effect as if they had been filed under § 1 605A. [9] It appears that finally adjudicated cases are not covered, in which case unsatisfied judgments against Libya and its officials will likely be unenforceable. [10] Claimants do not appear to have any recourse in court to dispute the amount or a denial of compensation, although a claim against the United States for an uncompensated "taking" in violation of the Fifth Amendment would not be foreclosed.

REFERENCE

[1] The list, established by the State Department, currently includes Cuba, Iran, North Korea, Sudan, and Syria. Iraq was removed from the list in 2004; Libya was removed in 2006. North Korea is eligible to be removed from the list in August 2008 depending on progress in dismantling its nuclear program.

[2] TRIA § 201(d)(2) defines "blocked asset" to mean property seized or frozen pursuant to certain sanctions, but not property that may be transferred pursuant to a license that is required by statute *other than* the International Emergency Economic Powers Act (IEEPA) or the United Nations Participation Act of 1945. It also excludes diplomatic or consular property being used solely for diplomatic or consular purposes from the definition of "blocked asset." TRIA does not refer to regulated assets, so it is unclear whether "blocked" and "regulated" are mutually exclusive terms, or whether "blocked" assets would be considered to be "regulated" as well. Assets regulated pursuant to IEEPA presumably mean those that are licensed for transfer.

[3] *See* Plaut v. Spendthrift Farms, 514 U.S. 211 (1995).

[4] Presidential Determination No. 2008-9 of January 28, 2008, Waiver of Section 1083 of the National Defense Authorization Act for Fiscal Year 2008, 73 Fed. Reg. 6,571 (2008) (waiving all provisions of § 1083 with respect to Iraq).

[5] Acree v. Republic of Iraq, 370 F.3d 41 (D.C. Cir. 2004), *cert. denied*, 544 U.S. 1010 (2005). The district court rejected recently the plaintiffs' motion to reopen the case. Acree v. Iraq, 2008 WL 2764858 (D.D.C. 2008).

[6] Simon v. Iraq, 529 F.3d 1187 (D.C. Cir. 2008).

[7] Correspondence from the U.S.-Libya Business Association, the National Foreign Trade Council, the National Association of Manufacturers, and the United States Chamber of Commerce to U.S. Secretary of State Condoleezza Rice, February 28, 2008 (urging the Administration to seek waiver authority with respect to Libya). For more information about U.S.-Libya relations, see CRS Report RL33142, *Libya: Background and U.S. Relations*, by Christopher M. Blanchard.

[8] 28 U.S.C. § 1605A provides a cause of action for "personal injury or death," which appears to cover a broader scope of injuries than "wrongful death or physical injury." Claims for wrongful death under the FSIA amendment have been limited to the decedent's estate, while close relatives of a victim have recovered in their own right based on claims of solatium, intentional

infliction of emotional distress, and pain and suffering, depending on the applicable state law. *See, e.g.*, Pugh v. Libya, 530 F. Supp. 2d 216 (D.D.C. 2008).

[9] NDAA § 1083(c) provides that pending cases originally brought under previous 28 U.S.C. § 1605(a)(7) are to be given effect as if they had been filed under § 1605A if the action was "adversely affected on the grounds that [the previous] provisions fail to create a cause of action against the state" and the plaintiff makes a motion to the court asking for such treatment.

[10] Price v. Libya, 384 F. Supp. 2d 120 (D.D.C. 2005)(approximately $18 million judgment against Libya for injuries suffered during plaintiffs' imprisonment pending trial for allegedly taking unlawful photographs); Pugh v. Libya, 530 F. Supp. 2d 216 (D.D.C. 2008)(nearly $7 billion judgment against Libya and six named officials for bombing of a French airliner over Africa in 1989).

INDEX

A

ad hoc, 16
adjudication, 23
administration, 68
administrative, 5, 18
adult, 19
Afghanistan, 28, 29
Africa, 58, 96, 107
agent, 6, 7, 19, 37, 38, 61, 72, 77, 85, 90
agents, vii, 1, 2, 7, 20, 23, 27, 31, 34, 37, 38, 48, 50, 51, 75, 79, 85, 86, 100, 105
aid, vii, 2, 9, 17, 37, 39, 40, 42, 44, 48, 80, 91, 101, 102, 103
air, 2
Airlines, 72
Al Qaeda, 29
alienation, 40, 102
alternative, 3, 10, 12, 18, 71
alternatives, 33
alters, 82
amendments, 4, 10, 24, 37, 44, 51, 63, 73, 78, 82, 92, 101
anti-terrorism, 32, 83, 104
application, 15, 20, 22, 28, 39, 45, 70, 78, 89, 93
appropriations, 9, 10, 14, 22, 24, 66, 76
appropriations bills, 24
Appropriations Committee, 24, 66, 76
arbitration, 36, 47, 63, 65
argument, 35, 36, 77, 83, 92
Armed Forces, 34, 38, 80, 84
Army, 91
arrest, 50
assassination, 34, 78
assessment, 35
assets, vii, viii, 1, 2, 3, 4, 6, 7, 8, 9, 10, 11, 12, 14, 15, 17, 18, 24, 25, 26, 27, 28, 29, 30, 31, 33, 34, 35, 36, 37, 41, 42, 43, 44, 49, 51, 52, 55, 58, 59, 65, 67, 71, 78, 80, 81, 82, 83, 89, 91, 92, 97, 99, 100, 101, 103, 104, 106
attachment, vii, viii, 1, 2, 8, 9, 10, 11, 12, 14, 17, 33, 35, 37, 39, 40, 42, 43, 44, 46, 48, 59, 65, 67, 71, 80, 82, 83, 87, 89, 91, 92, 99, 100, 101, 102, 104
attacks, 3, 16, 29, 52, 79
Attorney General, 28, 62
authority, viii, 8, 9, 10, 14, 17, 20, 22, 26, 27, 32, 34, 35, 38, 42, 43, 46, 65, 66, 67, 70, 78, 84, 89, 95, 99, 101, 102, 106
availability, vii, 1, 20

B

bank account, 65
Bank of England, 90
banking, 35
banks, 90
barrier, 41, 52, 77, 104
battery, 88
benefits, 18, 42, 102
bilateral relations, 9
bilateral trade, 47, 105
binding, 77

bomb, 68, 69
breaches, 23
Bush Administration, 17, 18, 47, 105

C

capacity, 20, 27, 45, 58, 75, 79
Catholic, 69
CBS, 30
Central Bank, 33, 35, 81, 89
certification, 48
Chief Justice, 4
children, 19, 24, 30, 69
CIA, 72, 88
citizens, 11, 22, 29, 50, 63, 67, 72, 80, 85
civil action, 25
civilian, 2, 78, 80
Clinton Administration, 7, 8, 10, 12, 18
Co, 62, 75, 88, 90, 91
collateral, 35, 44, 103
Columbia, 19, 21, 22, 23, 39, 73, 96
commerce, 5
Committee on the Judiciary, 68
Committees on Appropriations, 46
common law, 19, 30, 75
community, 33
compensation, vii, 2, 3, 4, 10, 11, 12, 15, 16, 17, 18, 25, 28, 34, 36, 37, 47, 48, 49, 51, 58, 74, 95, 96, 105
competition, 5, 104
complexity, 51
compliance, 40, 51
confidence, 5
conflict, 77
Congress, vii, viii, 1, 2, 3, 5, 6, 7, 9, 10, 12, 13, 14, 15, 16, 18, 19, 21, 22, 23, 24, 25, 26, 27, 28, 32, 34, 37, 38, 45, 46, 47, 48, 49, 50, 51, 59, 63, 65, 68, 70, 71, 73, 74, 75, 76, 77, 78, 80, 82, 83, 94, 95, 96, 97, 99, 100, 101, 103, 105
Congressional Budget Office, 12
Connecticut, 87
consent, 4, 50
Consolidated Appropriations Act, 7, 46
consolidation, 32, 33

Constitution, 9
construction, 77
Consumer Price Index, 37
contractors, 13, 38, 78
contracts, 13, 23, 95
control, 2, 42, 83, 84, 86, 90, 102
conversion, 33
corporations, 12, 96
costs, 39
counsel, 78
counterterrorism, 33
Court of Appeals, 2, 3, 19, 23, 27, 29, 30, 67, 100
courts, vii, viii, 1, 2, 3, 4, 5, 6, 7, 12, 13, 15, 19, 21, 22, 28, 34, 37, 38, 40, 41, 42, 43, 44, 45, 48, 51, 61, 62, 63, 67, 71, 76, 77, 78, 83, 85, 86, 88, 89, 93, 94, 99, 103
coverage, 38
credit, 47
creditors, viii, 4, 14, 29, 33, 41, 44, 51, 58, 67, 74, 78, 82, 90, 97, 99, 101
criticism, 3, 89
CRS, viii, 1, 59, 95, 96, 99, 100, 106
Cuba, viii, 7, 8, 10, 11, 12, 13, 14, 50, 58, 62, 64, 65, 66, 67, 71, 75, 88, 89, 90, 96, 97, 99, 106
Cuban government, 13, 97
currency, 86

D

death, 5, 6, 34, 37, 38, 48, 49, 50, 61, 63, 74, 85, 96, 105, 106
debt, 44, 45, 90
debts, 11, 12, 35, 43, 47, 55, 104
decisions, vii, 2, 8, 44
defendants, vii, 1, 29, 33, 40, 75, 93
defense, 7, 27, 84, 95
defenses, 44, 45, 81, 103
definition, 51, 72, 80, 84, 92, 106
delivery, 36, 41, 47, 84
democracy, 32, 33
denial, 49, 105
Department of Defense, 22, 70, 76
Department of Justice, 28, 62, 63

Index

Department of State, 22, 62, 63, 95, 96
destroyers, 70
detention, 70, 76
dignity, 5
disabled, 94
discretionary, 45
disposition, 73
disputes, 5, 8, 47, 67
distress, 19, 20, 30, 49, 96, 107
distribution, 74
District of Columbia, 19, 21, 22, 23, 39, 73, 96
due process, 35, 41, 45, 88, 103
duties, 80, 82

E

economic damages, 20, 37, 38, 61
economic development, 32
economic security, 101
ego, 42, 90
Emergency Supplemental Appropriations Act, 66
emotion, 51
emotional, 19, 20, 30, 49, 77, 96, 107
emotional distress, 19, 20, 30, 49, 96, 107
employees, vii, 1, 7, 19, 23, 27, 37, 38, 48, 51, 75, 79, 85, 100, 105
employers, 80
employment, 5, 6, 7, 19, 33, 37, 38, 61
energy, 46
England, 8, 90
entanglement, 81
enterprise, 5
equality, 4, 5
estimating, 69
Eureka, 94
evolution, vii, 2
execution, 9, 17, 34, 36, 37, 39, 41, 42, 43, 48, 61, 63, 71, 80, 83, 86, 87, 91, 92, 93, 101, 102, 104
Executive Branch, 75
Executive Order, 65
exercise, 5, 6, 10, 32, 34, 41, 45, 77, 80, 103
expert, 80

F

failure, 19, 27, 30, 31
fairness, 51
faith, 46
false imprisonment, 50
family, 16, 24, 28, 37, 49, 64, 69, 72, 79, 80, 85, 88
family members, 24, 28, 37, 49, 79, 80, 85
fear, 30, 80
February, 12, 29, 81, 89, 95, 96, 106
federal courts, 63, 78, 94
federal government, 15
federal law, 40
Federal Reserve, 29, 65, 79, 80
Federal Reserve Bank, 29, 65, 79, 80
Fidel Castro, 65, 75, 88
Fifth Amendment, 49, 105
finance, 33, 46
financial institution, 47
financial institutions, 47
financial loss, 50
financial resources, 32
financing, 19, 70
fines, 37
flight, 72
Foreign Military Sales, 12, 13, 14, 44, 55, 70
foreign nation, 45, 67
foreign nationals, 45
foreign policy, 3, 8, 18, 51, 65, 67
foreigners, 81
Fox, 91
fraud, 88, 92, 94
freezing, 81
funds, 2, 3, 8, 10, 13, 14, 15, 25, 27, 28, 29, 30, 32, 35, 37, 39, 44, 46, 48, 49, 51, 65, 74, 84, 92, 101, 105

G

Gaza, 64
Gaza Strip, 64
genocide, 63
goals, 3, 18, 51

Index

good faith, 46
goods and services, 13
government, 2, 3, 6, 7, 8, 12, 13, 15, 19, 21, 22, 24, 25, 26, 27, 30, 33, 34, 35, 38, 42, 43, 45, 46, 48, 50, 59, 61, 62, 65, 74, 75, 79, 84, 86, 90, 91, 92, 97, 100, 101, 102, 104, 105
grants, 84
groups, 72
growth, 47, 105
Gulf War, 26, 28, 104

H

Hamas, 68, 71
harm, 32, 47, 105
hearing, 18, 21, 27, 68, 88
Hezbollah, 19, 49, 64, 68, 69, 72
Holland, 93
hospital, 88
hostage, 2, 6, 8, 11, 18, 19, 21, 22, 24, 25, 29, 30, 37, 39, 49, 64, 66, 72, 77, 78, 80, 100
hostage taking, 2, 6, 100
hotels, 81
House, 10, 12, 16, 23, 28, 32, 38, 62, 63, 64, 66, 67, 68, 70, 73, 79, 82, 95, 104
human, 30, 50, 81
human rights, 50

I

id, 3, 7, 26, 67, 68, 75, 80, 82, 94
identification, 17
identity, 48
immunity, vii, 2, 3, 4, 5, 7, 8, 11, 21, 22, 24, 26, 27, 29, 31, 32, 33, 35, 36, 38, 42, 43, 44, 46, 48, 58, 61, 62, 74, 75, 77, 80, 82, 83, 84, 86, 87, 89, 90, 91, 92, 95, 100, 102, 105
imprisonment, 26, 50, 96, 107
independence, 4, 5
indexing, 40
indication, 75
inflation, 74

injuries, 2, 28, 50, 63, 71, 74, 85, 96, 105, 106, 107
injury, 5, 6, 37, 38, 48, 49, 50, 61, 63, 76, 96, 105, 106
institutions, 47
instruments, 40, 47, 83
insurance, 38
intangible, 86
intelligence, 34, 61
interference, 50, 66
International Chamber of Commerce, 34
international law, 4, 30, 63
international terrorism, 11, 15, 16, 18, 32, 39
interpretation, 19, 20, 24, 33, 44, 48, 83, 87
intervention, 26, 46, 50
intrinsic, 86, 93
investment, 47, 105
Iran, vii, viii, 2, 4, 7, 8, 10, 11, 12, 13, 14, 15, 16, 17, 18, 19, 21, 22, 23, 24, 25, 27, 34, 35, 36, 37, 39, 44, 49, 50, 51, 55, 59, 61, 62, 64, 65, 66, 67, 68, 69, 70, 71, 73, 74, 75, 76, 77, 78, 84, 85, 86, 90, 91, 92, 93, 96, 99, 100, 101, 106
Iraq, vii, viii, 1, 2, 3, 4, 25, 26, 27, 28, 29, 30, 31, 32, 33, 34, 38, 42, 46, 50, 51, 58, 62, 72, 78, 79, 80, 81, 82, 83, 86, 89, 92, 95, 99, 101, 102, 104, 106
Iraq Relief and Reconstruction Fund, 29
Islamic, 4, 7, 16, 17, 21, 22, 27, 29, 34, 49, 61, 64, 65, 68, 69, 71, 73, 74, 75, 76, 77, 78, 84, 85, 86, 90, 92, 93
Israel, 68

J

Jerusalem, 71, 94
journalists, 30
judge, 19, 20, 29, 30, 36
judges, 20, 85
judgment, viii, 2, 4, 6, 7, 9, 10, 11, 13, 14, 17, 19, 21, 22, 23, 26, 27, 29, 30, 31, 33, 34, 35, 36, 39, 41, 42, 43, 44, 45, 46, 47, 49, 50, 51, 55, 58, 59, 61, 67, 71, 74, 78, 79, 82, 83, 86, 87, 88, 89, 90, 91, 92, 93, 94, 95, 96, 97, 99, 101, 102, 103, 107

Index

judicial power, 45, 103
Judiciary, 12, 15, 22, 63, 68, 76
Judiciary Committee, 12, 63, 68
jurisdiction, 3, 4, 5, 6, 7, 23, 25, 28, 30, 32, 33, 35, 37, 38, 45, 47, 52, 61, 62, 64, 73, 76, 77, 78, 88, 100
jurisdictions, 40
justice, 10, 71
Justice Department, 26, 27, 67

K

Kentucky, 75
kidnapping, 50
killing, 2, 6, 100
Korea, viii, 62, 99, 106
Kuwait, 29, 30, 72, 80, 81

L

language, 22, 25, 28, 35, 39, 42, 43, 44, 46, 49, 63, 78, 89, 100, 102
law, vii, 1, 2, 3, 4, 9, 10, 12, 14, 16, 17, 19, 20, 21, 22, 23, 26, 29, 30, 32, 38, 39, 40, 41, 45, 46, 47, 51, 63, 64, 67, 70, 71, 73, 74, 75, 77, 79, 82, 85, 89, 96, 101, 103, 104, 107
laws, 4, 10, 20, 37, 67, 91, 100
lawsuits, vii, viii, 1, 2, 3, 19, 29, 38, 39, 41, 46, 47, 48, 50, 51, 64, 100, 103, 105
Lebanon, 39, 64, 69, 72, 86
legislation, vii, viii, 2, 4, 9, 11, 12, 14, 15, 23, 24, 50, 63, 66, 71, 78, 95, 99
letters of credit, 47
Libya, vii, viii, 1, 2, 3, 46, 47, 48, 49, 50, 59, 62, 75, 89, 94, 95, 96, 99, 102, 105, 106, 107
lien, 39, 40, 41, 83, 87, 89, 92, 101
liens, 39, 40, 88
limitation, 20, 44, 45, 103
limitations, 19, 30, 39, 41, 44, 45, 52, 61, 63, 81, 85, 94, 102
liquidate, 13

litigation, 3, 18, 33, 37, 40, 41, 47, 68, 78, 81, 89, 102
lobbyists, 86
losses, 11, 38, 47
Louisiana, 20

M

macroeconomic, 33
maintenance, 33
marketing, 83
marriage, 88
measures, 40, 63, 87, 102
men, 30
Miami, 75, 88, 97
military, 13, 25, 35, 36, 61, 70, 80, 84, 88, 89
MOD, 2, 34, 35, 36, 61
money, 6, 13, 24, 35, 37, 38, 40, 43, 61, 63
moratorium, 30
motion, 21, 22, 23, 24, 26, 27, 30, 31, 44, 45, 90, 92, 93, 103, 106, 107

N

nation, 4, 5
National Defense Authorization Act, vii, viii, 1, 3, 31, 38, 81, 82, 90, 99, 101, 106
national emergency, 65
national security, 9, 11, 14, 17, 18, 32, 65, 67, 68, 71, 104
Navy, 16, 69, 70
neglect, 92
negotiating, 8
New York, 65, 79, 80, 91
Niger, 58
Nigeria, 90
Nixon, 80
NO, 81
normal, 5, 8
normalization, 11
North Korea, viii, 62, 99, 106
nuclear, 106
nuclear program, 106

O

obligation, 42
obligations, 5, 9, 11, 22, 23, 42, 44, 51, 67, 83, 100
OFAC, 55
Office of Foreign Assets Control (OFAC), 15, 16, 25, 55, 59, 74, 97
Office of Management and Budget, 69
Oklahoma, 31
omission, 74, 85
omnibus, 66
opposition, 3, 10
organization, 64
organizations, 17, 70
Overseas Private Investment Corporation, 12
oversight, 28
ownership, 42, 43, 90, 91

P

pain, 20, 37, 38, 61, 96, 107
paramilitary, 72
Paris, 34, 71
Pennsylvania, 19, 20
perception, 3
performance, 47
permit, 3, 19, 27, 33, 37, 40, 43, 44, 46, 47, 52, 67, 88, 89, 101
personal, 5, 6, 20, 35, 37, 38, 39, 58, 59, 61, 62, 63, 75, 86, 96, 101, 106
petroleum, 34, 83, 104
petroleum products, 34, 83, 104
photographs, 96, 107
PL, 45
plausibility, 83
police, 80
power, 12, 93, 94
powers, 45, 65, 78, 103
prejudice, 94
president, 80
President Bush, 15, 16, 17, 22, 25, 26, 27, 30, 32, 38, 78, 88, 101
President Clinton, 2, 9, 10, 12, 14, 67, 82, 102
pressure, 15
prisoners, 26, 28, 104
prisoners of war, 26, 28, 104
private, 3, 5, 18, 20, 27, 33, 45, 64, 70, 74, 75, 84, 100
private practice, 18
private sector, 33
profits, 42, 43, 102
program, 12, 13, 15, 18, 66, 106
promote, 32, 33, 104
property, 2, 3, 5, 6, 8, 9, 10, 11, 12, 13, 14, 17, 25, 33, 35, 36, 37, 38, 39, 40, 41, 42, 43, 44, 46, 48, 55, 58, 59, 61, 66, 67, 70, 73, 76, 82, 84, 86, 87, 88, 89, 90, 91, 92, 95, 96, 101, 102, 105, 106
property owner, 40, 87, 88
property rights, 87
proposition, 80
protection, 9, 34, 104
public, 9, 74
public safety, 74
Puerto Rico, 68, 88, 90, 91
punitive, 3, 6, 7, 13, 18, 19, 20, 21, 26, 29, 37, 38, 44, 55, 58, 61, 64, 68, 69, 71, 74, 75, 80, 81, 85, 93, 101, 103

R

race, 11
real estate, 40, 86, 87
real property, 40, 41, 59, 86, 87, 91
recognition, 89
reconstruction, 25, 28, 32, 38, 51, 104
recovery, 19
refuge, 80, 81
regulation, 43, 70
regulations, 8, 35, 37, 43, 50, 97, 100, 102
relationship, 33, 47, 90, 105
relatives, 11, 15, 79, 96, 106
resolution, 46
resources, 6, 32
responsibilities, 16, 23
Revolutionary, 93
risk, 8, 9, 11, 47, 52, 67, 81
risks, 89

Index

Robert Gates, 95

S

sabotage, 2, 6, 100
Saddam Hussein, 25, 26, 27, 28, 29, 34, 72, 80, 81, 104
safety, 74
salaries, 80
sanctions, 3, 8, 11, 41, 43, 50, 52, 83, 92, 97, 100, 102, 104, 106
satisfaction, vii, 1, 6, 13, 14, 25, 29, 31, 34, 35, 36, 46, 49, 51
savings, 43
scarcity, 3, 100
Secretary of Commerce, 79, 95
Secretary of Defense, 95
Secretary of State, 16, 34, 46, 48, 50, 78, 83, 95, 105, 106
Secretary of the Treasury, 12, 13, 24, 83
securities, 94
security, 9, 11, 14, 17, 18, 32, 40, 65, 67, 68, 71, 101, 104
seizure, 76, 87
Senate, 10, 12, 16, 18, 23, 24, 28, 38, 50, 63, 64, 66, 68, 70, 74, 76, 95
separateness, 90
separation, 23, 45, 77, 103
separation of powers, 23, 45, 77, 103
September 11, 16, 79
series, 1
services, 13, 47, 61, 70
settlements, 9, 48, 105
shares, 90, 91
Shiite, 16
siblings, 19, 88
signs, 47, 105
sites, 30, 81
Speaker of the House, 95
specificity, 40
sponsor, 6, 7, 16, 21, 32, 39, 41, 45, 46, 47, 61, 86, 88, 91, 105
stability, 32, 33
State Department, viii, 5, 6, 11, 18, 21, 46, 47, 62, 66, 67, 99, 106

state laws, 20, 100
state-owned, 90
state-owned banks, 90
statute of limitations, 30, 39, 44, 45, 52, 61, 63, 81, 85, 94
statutes, 19, 20, 40, 41, 66, 75, 77, 88
statutory, 14, 30, 45, 77, 91
stock, 86, 90
Sudan, viii, 62, 75, 93, 99, 106
suffering, 20, 28, 37, 38, 61, 96, 107
suicide, 69, 71, 94
suppliers, 70
Supreme Court, 2, 12, 20, 27, 31, 33, 34, 35, 36, 51, 61, 84, 89, 94
surprise, 92
Syria, viii, 62, 99, 106

T

takeover, 65
Taliban, 29
tangible, 39, 41, 86, 101
teaching, 69
Tehran, 22, 50, 76, 96
territorial, 5
territory, 4, 5, 6, 63
terrorism, vii, viii, 1, 2, 3, 4, 6, 7, 8, 9, 10, 11, 12, 14, 15, 16, 17, 18, 20, 21, 26, 27, 28, 30, 31, 32, 33, 34, 35, 37, 38, 39, 41, 42, 43, 45, 46, 47, 48, 51, 58, 59, 61, 62, 63, 66, 67, 68, 71, 79, 82, 83, 85, 86, 88, 91, 94, 95, 99, 100, 101, 102, 103, 104, 105
terrorist, vii, viii, 1, 2, 3, 4, 6, 7, 9, 10, 11, 14, 15, 16, 17, 18, 19, 20, 21, 23, 25, 26, 29, 30, 31, 34, 37, 38, 45, 46, 49, 50, 51, 52, 55, 63, 65, 67, 70, 75, 77, 79, 80, 89, 91, 92, 93, 94, 95, 99, 100, 101
terrorist acts, vii, viii, 1, 2, 23, 32, 34, 38, 46, 63, 95, 99, 100
terrorist attack, 3, 16, 20, 29, 45, 52, 79, 93
Terrorists, 10, 16, 19, 68
testimony, 68, 80
third party, 12, 19, 20, 34, 38, 43
threat, 46, 65
threats, 11

time, 2, 3, 4, 6, 8, 15, 21, 23, 24, 27, 29, 34, 45, 49, 52, 63, 64, 65, 66, 72, 77, 89, 92, 94, 103
title, 4, 14, 17, 24, 31, 38, 39, 40, 41, 45, 50, 61, 74, 84, 87, 101
tort, 20, 51
torture, 2, 6, 26, 28, 63, 70, 88, 100
trade, 33, 41, 46, 47, 52, 89, 104, 105
Trading with the Enemy Act, 8, 63
training, 33, 70
transactions, 40, 41, 47, 52, 65, 70, 82, 89, 102
transfer, 73, 106
Treasury, 9, 10, 11, 12, 13, 14, 15, 16, 24, 29, 36, 44, 59, 65, 66, 67, 68, 70, 74, 83, 92
Treasury Department, 9, 10, 13, 14, 29
trial, 7, 16, 18, 19, 21, 24, 63, 88, 92, 96, 107
tribunals, 55
trust, 13, 44
trust fund, 13, 44

U

U.S. Agency for International Development, 72
U.S. economy, 47, 105
U.S. Secretary of Commerce, 95
U.S. Treasury, 36, 44, 65, 92
uncertainty, 12, 51
uniform, 94
United Nations, 37, 69, 73, 92, 106
United States, vii, 2, 4, 5, 6, 7, 8, 9, 10, 11, 13, 14, 15, 17, 21, 22, 23, 24, 26, 28, 31, 32, 33, 34, 36, 37, 38, 39, 40, 44, 45, 47, 49, 50, 51, 52, 55, 59, 61, 63, 64, 65, 66, 67, 71, 73, 76, 77, 79, 81, 82, 83, 84, 86, 89, 92, 94, 95, 97, 101, 103, 104, 105, 106

V

validity, 22, 29, 31, 35, 66
values, 59
venue, 41
victims, vii, viii, 1, 2, 3, 4, 6, 8, 10, 11, 12, 14, 15, 16, 18, 25, 26, 28, 37, 39, 45, 46, 47, 48, 49, 50, 51, 59, 68, 71, 79, 95, 99, 100, 105
Victims of Trafficking and Violence Protection Act, 2, 4, 10, 12, 34, 74
Vietnam, 11
Violence Against Women Act, 10
vocational, 33
vocational training, 33
voice, 12, 16, 73

W

wages, 80
war, 26, 28, 65, 68, 104
war on terror, 68
White House, 32, 62, 67, 73, 79, 82, 104
White House Office, 67
wholesale, 11
winning, 100
wives, 30
women, 69
World Trade Center, 29
World War, 5
World War I, 5
World War II, 5